Is There a Tomorrow?
YES!

Temima Gezari

Published in Celebration of Her 98th Birthday

STUDIO WORKSHOP PRESS

IS THERE A TOMORROW? YES!

by Temima Gezari

Published by

Studio Workshop Press
66 Noah's Path
Rocky Point, NY 11778

631-744-2054

ISBN 0-9616269-5-X

First Edition – December 2003

All rights reserved
© 2003 by Studio Workshop Press

No part of the material protected by this notice may be reproduced or utilized in any form or by any means without written permission of the copyright owner.

Printed in the U. S. A.

Contents

Chapter 1 -	Off to the Land of Israel	1
Chapter 2 -	The Sabal	8
Chapter 3 -	A Land of Festivals	16
Chapter 4 -	The Meaning of a Tree	24
Chapter 5 -	More Adventures	29
Chapter 6 -	The Spirit of the People	33
Chapter 7 -	Exhibition on the Roof	36
Chapter 8 -	Homeward Via England	41
Chapter 9 -	New Opportunities	45
Chapter 10 -	The Synagogue Mural	49
Chapter 11 -	Another Mural Project	56
Chapter 12 -	Restoration	64
Chapter 13 -	Return to Kibbutz	66
Chapter 14 -	The Kibbutzniks	75
Chapter 15 -	Zvi	82
Chapter 16-	Painting in Mexico	86
Chapter 17 -	Return My Love	88
Chapter 18 -	A New Life Together	93

Biographical Sketch

Special thanks to Natalie Aurucci Stiefel for her untiring efforts and great generosity in contributing so much toward the production and publication of this book, and to Lyn Stevens for her valuable editorial assistance and continuing creative and literary support.

All artwork and photography reproduced in this book are by Temima Gezari

CHAPTER 1 – OFF TO THE LAND OF ISRAEL

My first trip to Israel, then Palestine, was in 1933. It was the Deep Depression and the United States was in the doldrums. Banks were failing. The wealthy, now penniless, were jumping out of windows. Men stood on street corners selling apples. When I was growing up in Brownsville, Brooklyn, everybody was poor. We immigrant kids worked out a very interesting life for ourselves. Though we had no money, we had plenty of imagination. It was fun. But now, as a young adult, I did not want to spend this important time of my life in the midst of such human tragedy. So I withdrew my meager savings from the bank before it could fail and set out to visit the land of the bible.

I was a young artist so, of course, I had to spend a few weeks enroute at the Louvre in Paris and similarly at museums in Italy, enjoying the great masterpieces that up to then I had known only from reproductions.

When I arrived in Jerusalem I found a little apartment on the roof of the last house in what was then, the last street of that ancient city. I was never so happy in my life – a large room full of sunlight, a separate toilet with a sink. I bought a cot, a primus gasoline stove for cooking. I built an easel, a table, chairs and bookshelves out of the many large wooden crates that first wave of Jews fleeing Germany, and the growing Nazi influence, had brought packed with their worldly goods.

One very important element was missing – a shower. Well, a little imagination solved that problem.

The Old City Of Jerusalem, 1934 (Jerusalem)

I bought a long rubber hose, attached a showerhead to it, screwed it on to the faucet in the sink and, voila! A shower. How about privacy on the roof? No problem. This was the last house on the last street. All you saw when you looked beyond the rooftop terrace was empty fields and desert for miles and miles. Every day an Arab Shepherd, watching his sheep, serenaded the vast emptiness with sweet music from his *halil* (flute).

Now I was ready to start work. I had no problem finding interesting subjects. The streets were swarming with workmen, mostly Arab, with their striped shirts and pantaloons. The donkeys stood by patiently waiting for their masters to load baskets of sand and stone to be delivered to some building site, of which there were many in this old but new land.

I filled my days with exploring, sketching and painting. I never had to go far. There, as I looked down from my roof, I saw a group of donkeys, loaded with baskets of stones and sand, one basket on each side of their firm little bodies and looking for all the world like a "Donkey Ballet." So that is what the completed composition, a pencil drawing became.

An Arab stonecutter, sitting in a group with his back to me and hammering away on a large rock to make stones of a required size, was a perfect example of a Bach fugue with variations on a theme. His rounded back resembled an egg, his sleeves, the same. His black turban, skillfully wound around his head, provided another egg shape. This became another pencil composition. Wherever I turned, there was another subject to draw or paint.

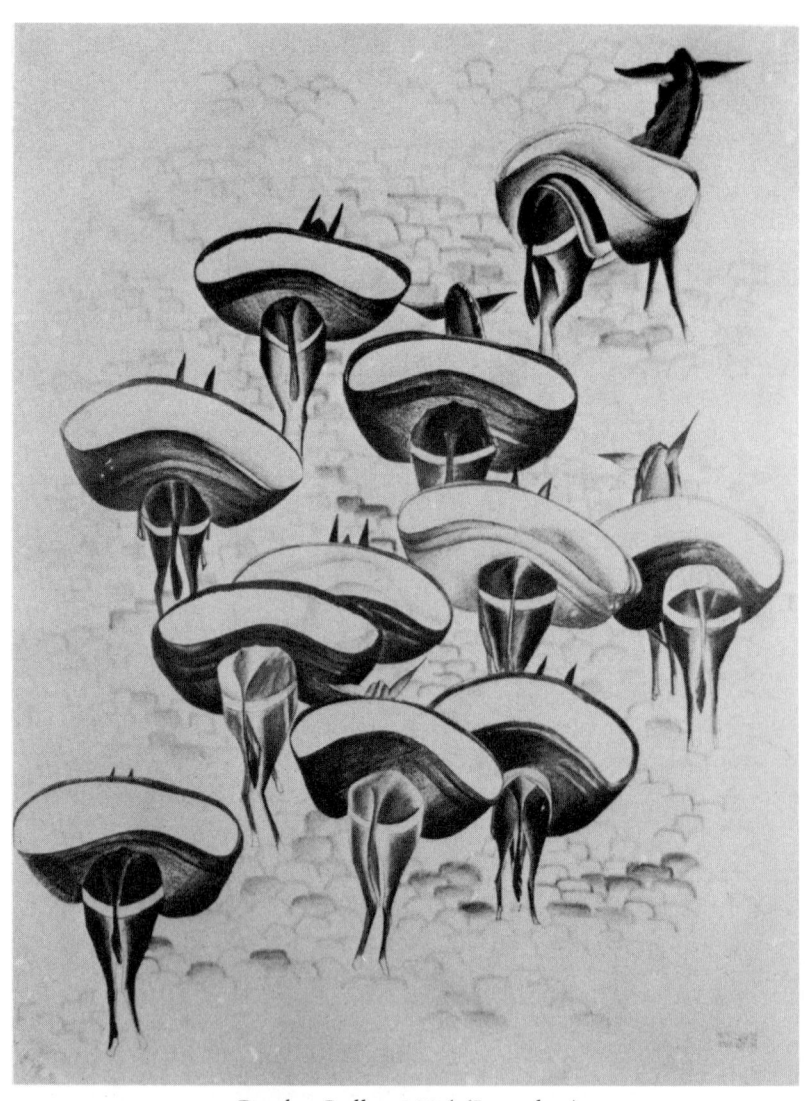

Donkey Ballet, 1934 (Jerusalem)

Temima in her Jerusalem studio (1934)

Stoneworkers

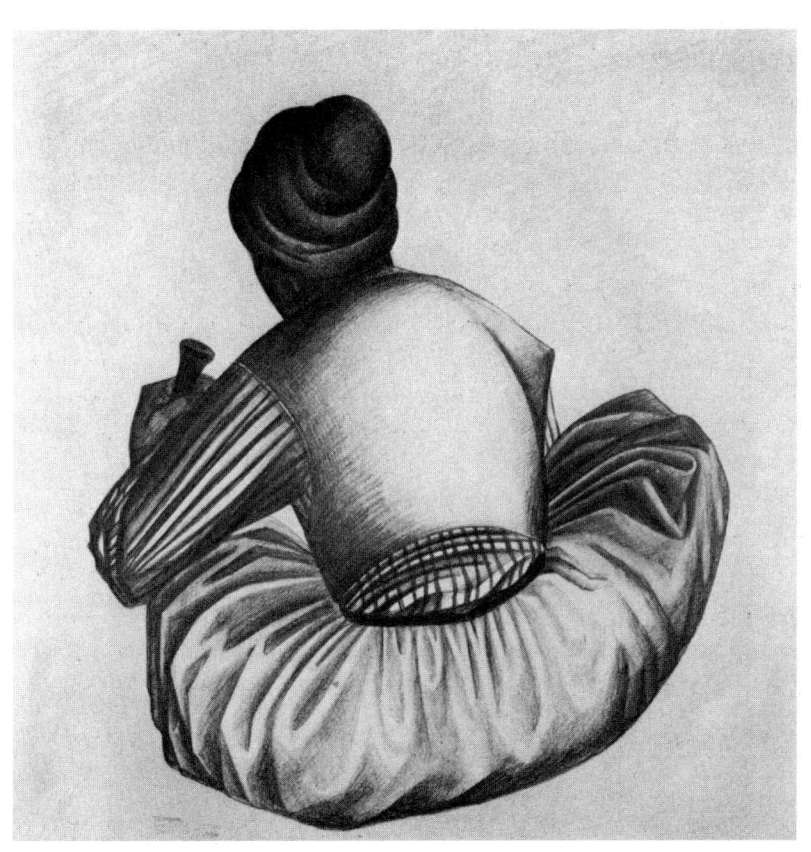

Arab Stone Cutter 1934 (Jerusalem)

CHAPTER 2 - THE SABAL

One day I was walking through a busy street in Jerusalem when I saw a *sabal* (porter) sitting on the curb. He was a Yemenite Jew who, with many of his countrymen, left Yemen for the Promised Land, now Israel. He was a very little man with delicate features, dressed in the garb of his trade – immediately recognizable by the coils of rope tied around his narrow waist. He may have been resting, or, more likely waiting for somebody to hire him to transport a bed, or a cupboard or a bulging sack, from one part of town to another. For this, he would receive a few *piastres*. I was fascinated with the manner with which a sabal would bind the object to his back with a rope across his forehead and, bending under the weight, would proceed barefoot to his destination with a nimble, running step.

I did not realize what problems would arise for me in trying to get this old sabal to pose for a drawing. When I approached him, he sprang to his feet and began to speak Hebrew in a strange accent as only a Yemenite would. Even though I understood Hebrew, it sounded like very foreign gibberish to me. My American Hebrew, I am sure, must have sounded equally strange to him. Apparently, at the end of our peculiar conversation, we both came away under two differing illusions - he, thinking that I wanted him to move something for me, and I, quite certain that he was willing to pose for me. I wrote my address on a card and gave it to him. From his constant nodding in agreement I gathered that he would be coming along very soon. He kept on repeating the word "*tekef*" which means "immediately" or "right

Sabal (Porter), 1938

away". I discovered later that here in Jerusalem it had the same connotation as "*manyana*" in Spanish.

I returned to my apartment elated, expecting a knock on my door any minute and the arrival of the most exotic model who ever posed for me. I stood on my roof looking in the direction from which he would appear. That day passed, and the next, and the next. Then, like a mirage in the desert, I saw the little, old Yemenite walking toward my house. Actually, he did not walk, but rather, ran along with short springing steps. Every so often, he stopped a passerby and pointed to the piece of paper I had given him a few days before. When the passerby waved in the direction of my house, the sabal resumed running until he passed another person, whom he stopped to ask directions again. The pantomime was repeated until, finally, he came within earshot and I called to him to climb the two flights to my apartment.

When he came into the room, he glanced around looking for whatever object that was to be moved. Was it the couch? the table? the easel? He turned to me every few steps. Is it this? This? This? My answer was that I asked him to sit down. He sat down on the floor perplexed. I gave him an orange. He began to peel it. I picked up my sketchpad and began to draw. It was very quiet. He was eating. I was drawing. Everything was perfect as far as I was concerned.

Suddenly, he realized what was happening and sprang up with a shout. What was I doing? I explained that I was drawing his picture to show to my parents in New York who had never seen a Yemenite Jew before. He shouted, "Don't you know that it is written in the

Torah that it is forbidden to make graven images?" With that he threw the unfinished orange on the floor and ran out of the room, scampering down the steps like a frightened rabbit. I ran after him, "But this is not a graven image. I am an art student, and I'm very anxious to study your beautiful head. I will pay you what you would earn for a whole day of hard work if you will just sit quietly for one hour while I make a few sketches." He shouted back, "Not even for a million pounds." As he dashed away he turned and spat, as though to avoid the plague.

I was shamed by this man's integrity and deep faith, and also inspired. I returned to my studio and made two drawings - one, a porter bent over by the load on his back - the second, the Sage, wise and serene, with a beautiful, flowing beard.

Day followed golden day. I spent many hours wandering through the Old City, enthralled by its ancient stone buildings, its winding, cobblestone alleys and crowded streets. Before me passed a continuous panorama of colorful humanity, representing seventy-five different nationalities, each claiming Jerusalem as its own.

The Wailing Wall, now called the Western Wall, had very limited space surrounding it at that time. Jews huddled close to it, praying silently or swaying back and forth and *davening* in the old, traditional manner. Bits of paper, with prayers and pleas for help of one kind or another were carefully folded and stuffed into the crevices between the ancient stones, with the hope that

The Sabal 1934

The Sage, 1934 (Jerusalem)

these letters would reach their divine destination and soon the prayers would be answered.

I never missed a day of sketching in the Old City. It was overwhelming; the donkeys, the camels, the crowds of people in native dress from all over the world, the colors of fruits and vegetables, the stalls filled with all kinds of wares, brass, copper, rugs, abayas, kefiyas, sandals, shoes, leather pouches, purses, belts, and things to eat; *humus, leben, meetz.* Then there were the sounds; the calls of the trades-people hawking their wears, the clatter of wheels on the cobblestones, the braying of donkeys, the shouting of their masters urging them along, "*Yallah! Yallah!,*" and the sounds of conversations in high and low keys and in numerous languages and accents. What an experience!

CHAPTER 3 – A LAND OF FESTIVALS

There were times, however, when I left the Old City. There were so many other places in the country to visit - especially on holidays. When *Purim* came, there was an excitement in the air. Tel Aviv was the host city for the celebration. So everybody packed a little suitcase and set out for Tel Aviv. They traveled every possible way; by car, (of which there were few), wagon, train and bus. Bus was definitely the way to go. The buses were filled to capacity. But that did not matter. People sat on seats or arms of seats, or on the floor. We talked to each other. After only brief conversation, we were on first name basis. We were family.

"Do you have friends in Tel Aviv? Where are you going to stay? You don t know anybody? Come with us. My cousin has plenty of room."

So it happened that complete strangers shared blankets on the floor of a house belonging to somebody s uncle, aunt, cousin or somebody else s uncle. What fun it was, and how meaningful to all of us! The family of Israel was living in the land of Israel.

Tel Aviv was a carnival. The whole city was decorated. I was impressed with the originality and creativity in a city that was going through pains of sudden growth. In just two decades Tel Aviv had grown from sand dunes and a few small houses, into a mini-metropolis. Now the streets were festooned with colorfully designed arches reaching from one side of the street to the other. The whole city was lavishly decorated.

The parade started. Purim characters in colorful, oriental costumes marched down the street while characters of the Megillah story followed, singing and dancing. Floats followed, beautifully designed and dealing with historical and contemporary characters cleverly exaggerated with much humor. There was singing, dancing and laughter. Everyone was in costume. I had never seen so many "Esthers", "Mordecais", "Hamans" and clowns at any one time. There was dancing in the streets all night, and three balls going on simultaneously in three different parts of the city. No one slept. It was a three day carnival. This was a Purim to remember!

Jerusalem was the host city for Passover, not only for us, but for the Christians who were celebrating Easter and the Arabs who were celebrating "Nebi Musa", (the prophet Moses). People from all over the land, as well as tourists and pilgrims from far away, crowded into Jerusalem, especially into the Old City. The city was ablaze with sunshine. The clarity of the sky bore promise of perfect weather for many months until the rain season would begin in December. Everybody was dressed in light, colorful, new, holiday clothes.

There had been much preparation for Passover. It was the same kind of excitement I remembered from my childhood, the excitement in Brownsville so many years before. Since most families were poor, it was not always possible to buy new pots and pans for the holiday. Also, much cooking during the year was done in copper pans and pots that had been brought over from the old country. In order to make them kosher for Passover, a very elaborate procedure took place. Metal pots were "*kashered*" by a process known in Yiddish, "*tzu veisen*". As a result of this mysterious process, which only my father knew, the copper pots emerged looking like new.

So, Jerusalem now was ready to celebrate the Festival of Freedom. The streets were filled to capacity with well dressed celebrants. The Jews prayed at the Wall. Christians attended special masses and followed the Stations of the Cross. Arabs danced sword dances, some being carried on the shoulders of others. All groups were celebrating this festival of spring, freedom and rejuvenation, in its own particular way. Some time later, I put much of this down in several drawings, which, today, bring back many happy memories. One thing is quite clear to me now – we were all celebrating the spring solstice.

Several weeks later, the *Lag B'Omer* festival was going to be observed in Meron, a small village in the hills in the north, not far from the ancient city of Safed. Some of my friends and I decided that we would drive up. We brought blankets with us because, even though it was May, it was still very cold at night and there was no hotel in which to spend the night. Everybody had to find a spot on the ground, spread a blanket or a heavy coat and somehow try to fall asleep. In planning for the trip, I decided to wear my riding habit, which I had found most convenient wearing apparel on a recent trip to a dig in Amman, Jordan.

Lag B'Omer means, "The thirty-third day of the counting of the Omer." The counting begins after the second *seder* at Passover and lasts for forty-nine days, exactly seven weeks, until *Shevuo*t, the harvest festival. Apparently, during the Roman invasion of Israel, the Jewish people were not permitted to study Torah. They were encouraged instead to participate in sports. The teachers and rabbinical scholars hid in caves in the forest in order to carry on their studying and teaching in safety. The students, pretending to spend the day hunting according to Roman decree, went out to the forest with bows and arrows. Instead of hunting, however, they spent the day studying with their teachers. Then a terrible plague spread among the students. Many died. However, the rejoicing was great when, on the thirty-third day of the counting of the Omer, the plague ended and the students returned to their studies. So *Lag B'Omer* has been celebrated through the centuries with outings and picnics in the woods.

In Israel there is an annual pilgrimage to Meron to celebrate the occasion at the tomb of Rabbi Shimon Bar Yochai, who participated in the Bar Kochba rebellion against the Romans. He was the author of the Zohar, the basic treatise on mysticism, which he wrote while hiding from the Romans. He was a contemporary of Rabbi Yochanon Ben Zakkai, the founder of the Academy at Yavneh which arose out of the ashes of the destruction of Jerusalem.

On the morning of the Lag B'Omer Festival, many buses and cars left Jerusalem in a long caravan for the trip north to Meron. Meanwhile, I had decided against going with my friends by car. I felt that I would be missing an important experience if I did not go by bus. The buses were full of Hassidim dressed in their holiday finery, singing and clapping hands. I was not going to miss that. So I boarded a bus and sat down next to a very happy *hassid*. I wore my riding outfit, trousers, mannish shirt and boots. In addition, those were the days of boyish hairstyles and I had one. I wore a small cap that an old, Arab woman had knitted for me on one of my many walks through the Old City. I also wore a simple camel s hair sport coat. My appearance completely confused my Hassidic companions. *"Is dus ah mansbil oder ah froyentsimmer?"* ("Is this male or female?")

My disguise seemed to work and I spent several hours singing, clapping hands and having a ball! I did not have to partake of the bottle being passed around, I was on a high of my own. However, there was one thing that confused me. Here were people, living in Jerusalem all their lives, singing over and over again, *"L' Shana Haba'ah b' Yerushalayim!"* (Next year in Jerusalem). Apparently, they were praying for the arrival of the Messiah when all good Jews would live in the land of Zion in peace and tranquility.

When we arrived in Meron, I found my friends, who were relieved to see me and anxious to hear about my bus ride. We explored the ancient structure nestling so comfortably on the hills not far from Safed, the seat of Mysticism. The building was teeming with Hassidim and tourists. There was a gallery where the women, children, bedding, food and stoves were all packed together. Below in the main court, a big bonfire had been lit. It was fed in a very unusual way. If you had a personal request of God, you simply took a personal item, like a handkerchief or a belt or kerchief, recited a prayer and threw the item into the fire. As you watched it being consumed, you were quite sure that your petition would be answered. So, if you were not married and wished that you would be, you followed this procedure. If, you were married but had no children, you followed the same procedure. All prayers would hopefully be answered the coming year. If not, there would be another opportunity next year.

This was the time of the haircutting ceremony. Little Orthodox boys, four or five years of age, all with long hair, straight or with curls down to their shoulders, lined up for their first manly haircut. Not all were delighted at the prospect, but tears and protests notwithstanding, prayers were recited, hair was clipped except for the *payot* (side locks), and the cuttings went into the flames with all the other personal items.

With fires burning and spirits high, the men began to sing and dance. They danced around the fire, the leaping flames reflected in their ecstatic faces. The women sat upstairs leaning over the rail enjoying their men s excitement from afar. The fiddle playing, the singing, the clapping of hands, the spirits, actual and ethereal, all this was too much for me. I decided to join the dancers. I was feeling very confident because of my successful bus trip. Who knows, maybe I have some hassidic genes in me from the distant past.

So I, a female, dressed like a boy, joined the ecstatic dancing men, against my friends warnings. This was unheard of, a woman dancing with the men?! What with the bottle being passed round and round, the inner ecstasy each dancer was experiencing, no one paid attention to me, dancing, clapping hands and having the time of my life. It was an experience never to be forgotten.

The *Shevuot* Festival, the "Feast of Weeks," came shortly after Lag B'Omer. This was the holiday of the first fruits of the harvest. In ancient times, the first fruits were brought to the temple as a sacrifice. Now in 1934, it was different, and how different it was. Again, the whole country packed a little bag and set out for Haifa, the host city for the big celebration. The city was decorated with greens in recognition of the third harvest festival, the other two being *Sukkot* and Passover. Garlands were hanging from the street lamps and criss-crossed from one side of the street to the other.

When the Shevuot parade began, it was gay and sunny, full of laughter and song. Along came the musicians followed by lines of children, dressed in white with garlands in their hair. They were carrying poles on which hung baskets filled with flowers or fruits or vegetables. After the little children passed by to the cheers of family and friends, came the older children some carrying flags and others carrying baskets full of produce. In addition, some children led lambs and goats, or carried sheaves of wheat, or containers of jams, jellies, cookies and other goodies.

When the parade came to an end, everybody turned in the direction of the Haifa Technion. Tables had been set up in the large courtyard there. As the children came in, they put their gifts on the tables. Then the fun began. People bought the various items and before an hour passed, the tables were all empty, and happy people left satisfied that besides having such a good time they had contributed handsomely to the *Keren Kayemet,* (the Jewish National Fund). All the money was going to be used for the redemption of the land.

This Shevuot parade was the subject of a mural that I was to paint in 1935 for the synagogue of Camp Cejwin.

CHAPTER 4 – THE MEANING OF A TREE

Another festival, very different from any of the others, took place shortly after Hanukkah. It was *Tu B Shevat* (Arbor Day) when the school children dressed in shorts, overalls and other work clothes, carrying pails of water, shovels, and boxes full of young saplings, marched to spots set aside for planting. The adults stood along the side of the road watching while the children of all ages spread over a barren field in Talpiot, a suburb of Jerusalem. Small groups of children worked together. Some dug, some planted, some watered. When the children stood back, it was like a miracle. What had but a short time before been a barren, dried out, ugly field was transformed into a miniature forest of saplings bearing promise of future forests and shaded woodlands. For more than a half century, tree planting has been a way of life in Israel and the results are spectacular. To see the pink almond tree in full bloom at this time is a perennial joy. The hillsides are dotted with red, yellow and lavender wildflowers. Nature is smiling and everyday cares are almost forgotten.

I have often wondered what the Israel Arbor Day means to children here in America. In Israel, of course, it is the time for planting trees, of studying Israel s flora and fauna, of the purposeful parades of the school children out to some barren slope. These stories we tell our children here, but still it is not their experience. For city children, especially, it is difficult to become enthusiastic over a holiday of planting, which happens to fall in midwinter, the bleakest and most colorless time of the year here in America. Enthusiasm has to be artificially stimulated through paying for a tree to be planted some six thousand miles away in Israel.

Yet, I am convinced that Tu Bishevat can mean something in addition to all this. It is interesting, with eyes covered, to go out, in imagination, in search of a tree we ourselves once met. We find out quickly that trees have meant different things to us at different ages. When we were infants, a tree served as a blurry background through which bits of blue sky or splotches of sunlight came trickling between such times as mommy s face appeared with a smile, with nourishment, or with a dangling toy. And when the smiling face withdrew, one could spend long moments between sleep watching with much fascination the leaves swaying back and forth to the rhythm of a gentle breeze.

When we were one or two years old, a tree was something to hold on to during those difficult months of trial and error when each step one took was a great adventure. Will I make it, or won't I? At the age of three or so we thought of a tree as part of a peek-a-boo game. For a five or six year old, a tree is really made for climbing.

As the years roll by, a tree becomes meaningful because of its shade and privacy, a place to sit with one s beloved. And later new young mothers sit on a bench under the tree chatting and laughing and exchanging confidences as they watch their babies sleeping peacefully in their perambulators. With later years, a tree is good to lean against in deep meditation. For old age, a tree

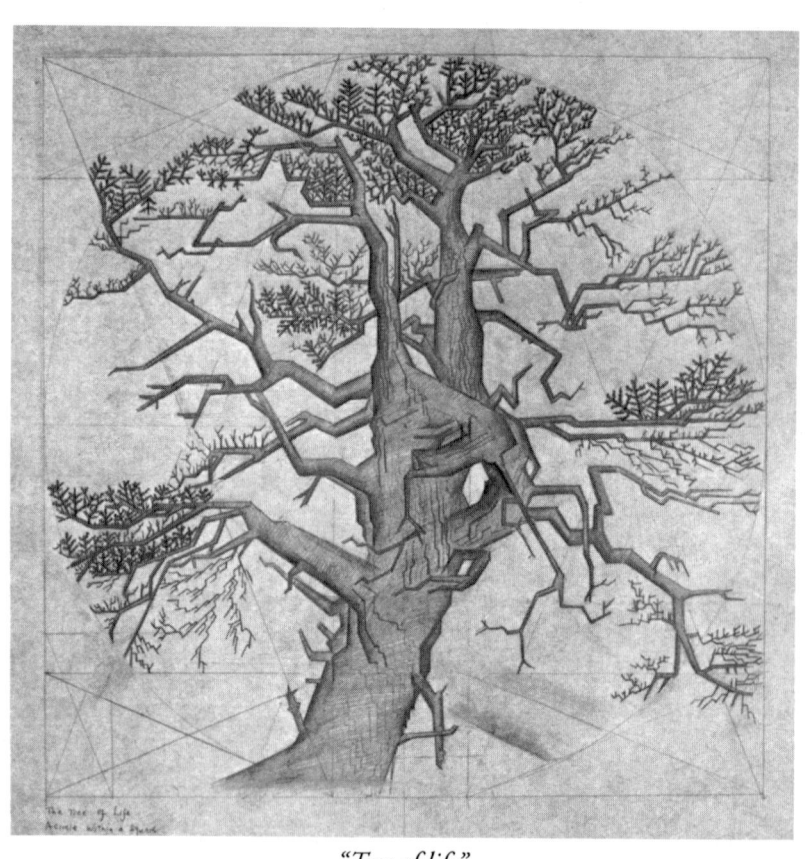

"Tree of life"

means peace and quiet and a comfortable vantage point from which to watch life pass by.

Occasionally I tried this exercise of going back in memory with my students, and highly personal trees began to appear. One student remembered a picnic in the woods. This happened somewhere in Eastern Europe. The morning had been full of gaiety and excitement. The woods rang with young shouts and laughter as the youths played games and went on a treasure hunt. The trees were tall and strong and beautiful, at the peak of their full summer foliage. Then, the student related, he wandered off in quest of a clue to a hidden treasure. He suddenly found himself alone in a dense part of the forest. Generations of pine needles lay on the ground, deadening the sound of his footsteps even to himself. He called. A dead silence was his answer. He called again and again. Panic stricken, he frantically looked up toward the sky. He could barely see any light through the fullness of the foliage overhead. The trees were tall, strong, menacing. They hemmed him in on all sides. There seemed to be no escape. Only more and more tall trees, with gnarled roots over which he stumbled and fell in the frantic search for his companions. When they found him, he was completely exhausted and faint with fear and panic. Youth heals quickly and in a short time he was playing games again, singing songs and enjoying the trees, so tall and strong and beautiful at the peak of their full summer foliage.

Then there was the tree which had a little lookout platform built by a father with keen insight. That tree went through many transformations with the young boy who climbed up to follow the beckoning finger of adventure. He told of the pirate ships he spied from his high vantage point, of the way he flapped his eagle wings as he in his regal role surveyed his kingdom from the highest mountain peak, or the way the tree served as a wonderful take-off for his plane that could fly at his mere wish, to any part of the universe.

CHAPTER 5 - MORE ADVENTURES

Time was passing quickly. I was painting every day. Wherever I turned, there was another subject. There were also trips to explore the cities, kibbutzim, Arab villages as well as trips to Egypt, Jordan, Lebanon and Syria. I generally went on these trips with a friend, Shoshanna, who joined me on a trip to Damascus and Beirut. She had been a French major in college. However, even though she could read volume after volume in French, she would not speak French. This gave me confidence in my limited two year high school French course, because I could speak French rather fluently. I felt that by pooling our French knowledge, whatever it was, we could get through the French speaking countries very easily. So on we went to Damascus.

The oriental bazaars in Damascus were very exciting. The strange costumes, the strange language, the motley crowds, the trades people in their stalls hawking their wares. We were always followed by groups of ragamuffins tugging at our garments, begging for coins. Whenever we stopped at a stall to buy something, a crowd immediately gathered to see what these Americans were interested in.

At one of the stalls I bought a man's brocade bathrobe magnificently woven with black, gold and silver threads. The inside was much more interesting than the outside. So when I returned to the U.S. months later, I turned the bathrobe inside out and front to back and made it into the most exotic outfit for formal occasions. A few years later, when fashions changed, I cut off twenty-four inches and wore it with a long, slim, black skirt. Then came the time when I converted it into a short blouse, still worn with a long, black skirt. This was my favorite outfit whenever I went out to lecture. Invariably, after the lecture, people, especially women, would surround me, showering me with compliments. "That was a wonderful lecture. Where did you buy that blouse?"

From Syria we planned to go on to Beirut. The only way to travel was by special car. When we got into the car, there was another passenger in it already. He was well groomed, dressed in an expensive business suit and wearing a fez, the usual headgear worn by government officials. We exchanged introductions. His card read "Minister of the Interior." We conversed in French. And who was carrying on the conversation? I, of course, with my two years of high school French. What courage! What nerve! It was a long, hot ride in that taxi over the picturesque, rugged Anti-Lebanon mountain range.

Tired, we stopped for a rest at a most delightful roadside inn. It was situated along a rushing brook over which a rustic wood bridge had been built. On the bridge were several small tables covered with colorful tablecloths and fresh flowers. We sat at a table overhung with blossoms from an overhead vine. A large bowl was set on the table. It was full of the largest, ripest strawberries we had ever seen. The minister of the interior was very gallant. He speared the strawberries with a little silver fork, rolled each in sugar and

Zoological Gardens — The Nile — Cairo, Egypt —

presented them to Shoshana and me, to our delight. It was an idyllic setting, full of pleasantness and friendliness.

Then, it was on to Beirut. We stayed at a newly built hotel. When the manager looked through my passport, he said to me. "I see you are an artist. I wonder if you could help us. As you see, we have opened this beautiful, new hotel, but we don't know how to make the rooms attractive to Americans. Would you be willing to mix colors and give suggestions to our painters and decorators?"

So, I became an interior decorator. It was fun! There I was, surrounded by dozens of tubs full of paint of every color imaginable. The hotel workmen helped with the mixing, pouring a little of this and a little of that into an empty tub until I got the color I wanted. The manager was so grateful that he treated Shoshana and me to dinner and then, with a friend, took us to a nightclub where we saw enough exotic belly dancers to last us for a lifetime.

CHAPTER 6 – THE SPIRIT OF THE PEOPLE

Back to Jerusalem and to work. Time was getting shorter and there was still so much to see and do. The Labor Day, May First holiday arrived. There was going to be a giant rally and celebration by workers at the Dead Sea. It was going to take place at night because of the intense heat during the day. So, at sundown, we crowded into buses rocking with song and laughter all the way.

When we arrived at the Dead Sea, the sun had set and it was pleasantly warm. A full moon was reflected in the quiet water. Everybody was in good mood. Every kind of work group was represented: Arab workers, Jewish workers, workers from the cities and from the kibbutzim. There were speeches and enthusiastic singing of labor songs in all languages. There was dancing of the *"hora"* by Jews and Arabs and of the *"debka"* by Arabs and Jews.

Everybody was a *chaver*, a comrade. I looked at an Arab sitting next to me, singing and clapping hands. His face was dark with strong features. If I had passed him o he street, I would have tried to leave lots of space between him and me. He looked so fierce. However, here, he was a comrade, and all differences melted quickly away.

The trip back to Jerusalem started out with singing, but soon it became quiet. It was three a.m. I looked out of the window. The full moon was shining on the Judaean Hills and caused deep shadows, which traced wonderful designs everywhere. The beauty was incredible.

When we arrived in Jerusalem, everybody disbanded. I, alone, was from Kerem Avraham. Well, what do you know? The bus driver, Moshe instead of leaving the bus in the bus terminal, drove me home. Nobody was out in the street at that hour. If there had been anyone, they would not have believed their eyes. Egged buses were never seen in that neighborhood. I realized that this consideration for a person was one of the beauties of this new land. I did not go to sleep but stayed up the rest of the night working on some compositions that became an important part of my growing body of work.

Something happened a short time later that further excited my enthusiasm for the new land. There had opened an Industrial Fair on the outskirts of the city. I waited at the bus stop for the special bus assigned to go to that new section of the city. I was sitting on a bench waiting. Then the bus arrived and we were off. Not until we approached the fair did I realize that I had left my bag with all my important papers, and my purse with all my money, on the bench where I had been waiting. The bus driver was most reassuring. "*Gevirty*," (Miss), don't worry, we will pick it up later when we return."

I must say that I did not enjoy that fair as much as I would have if my vision of an impending disaster were not so imminent. Words cannot express my delight and wonder when the bus pulled up at the bus stop and there was my bag, on the bench, just as I had left it, unopened. Where in the world could it have happened?

In a few weeks I was going to leave this land that I had become so accustomed to. I was now speaking Hebrew with the new Sephardic accent. When I arrived originally, I did not open my mouth to speak Hebrew because we had been taught only the Ashkenazic accent in America. For three weeks I listened but then I began to speak and was delighted when the tradespeople understood me. I gained confidence and could speak freely by the time I was ready to leave.

CHAPTER 7 – EXHIBITION ON THE ROOF

Time was rapidly coming for my departure. First, however, I wanted to have an exhibition. The only art gallery in Jerusalem was in a bookstore on Jaffa Road. The owner was very pleasant, but when I heard that the cost of a two week exhibition was equal to what it cost me to live in Jerusalem for two months, it was out of the question. I would have an exhibition - but of a different kind. So, I sent an announcement of my exhibition to "The Palestine Post" and another to the popular Hebrew newspaper, "Davar," saying that the exhibition would take place on two weekends, Saturday and Sunday afternoon at 4 p.m., on the roof of my house, at #9 Geulah Street in Kerem Avraham. I was excited at the prospect of having such a different kind of a show.

In recent years, we have been reading about a new trend in the field of art in New York. Artists are rebelling against the sky- high costs of having a show in a gallery. So, more and more, we see advertisements announcing studio exhibitions by artists. It is really a wonderful way of showing your work. Visitors enjoy the intimacy of seeing artists, on their own turf, of asking questions and getting direct answers from the artist without "benefit" of an intermediary in the form of a dealer or the owner of an art gallery. In 1934 I had unknowingly pioneered an approach to exhibits, which would not make an appearance until about forty years later.

The first day of the exhibition arrived. I had prepared very carefully for this special event, my first one-woman show. I had washed down the roof, spread blankets and cushions around and on the ledges and set out chairs, stools and a table for refreshments. Dragging my easel out on the roof was difficult, but there it was standing in the only shady spot I could find, with all my paintings and drawings neatly stacked next to it turned with their backs to the audience. On a long table were pitchers of fresh fruit drinks, bowls of nuts, raisins, figs, dates, all in season. What a spread!

Now the audience began to arrive. As I looked down the street, I saw them coming, individuals, couples, families dressed in their Shabbat best. After a quiet Shabbat morning, they were ready for some culture. What could be more interesting than this unusual exhibition by a young American who, they heard, had been living and painting for almost a year in Kerem Avraham.

In order to reach Kerem Avraham, one had to pass through Meiyah Shearim, a section of Jerusalem inhabited exclusively by the most orthodox Hassidim. Walking through those streets on the Shabbat was an extraordinary experience. The severe, heavy black coats on the hottest summer days did not seem to bother them. Women wore dresses with long sleeves and high necks, reaching down to their ankles. Of course, they all wore the ritual *sheitel* (wig) and a scarf to cover the wig. It seems that when the Jews lived in Poland, it was customary for the wives of wealthy Jewish merchants to visit Paris occasionally. When they returned, they brought with them news of the latest happenings in the great city. All the Parisian society ladies were wearing wigs, elaborate white wigs. So white wigs began to appear in the homes of the wealthy Jews in Poland. It

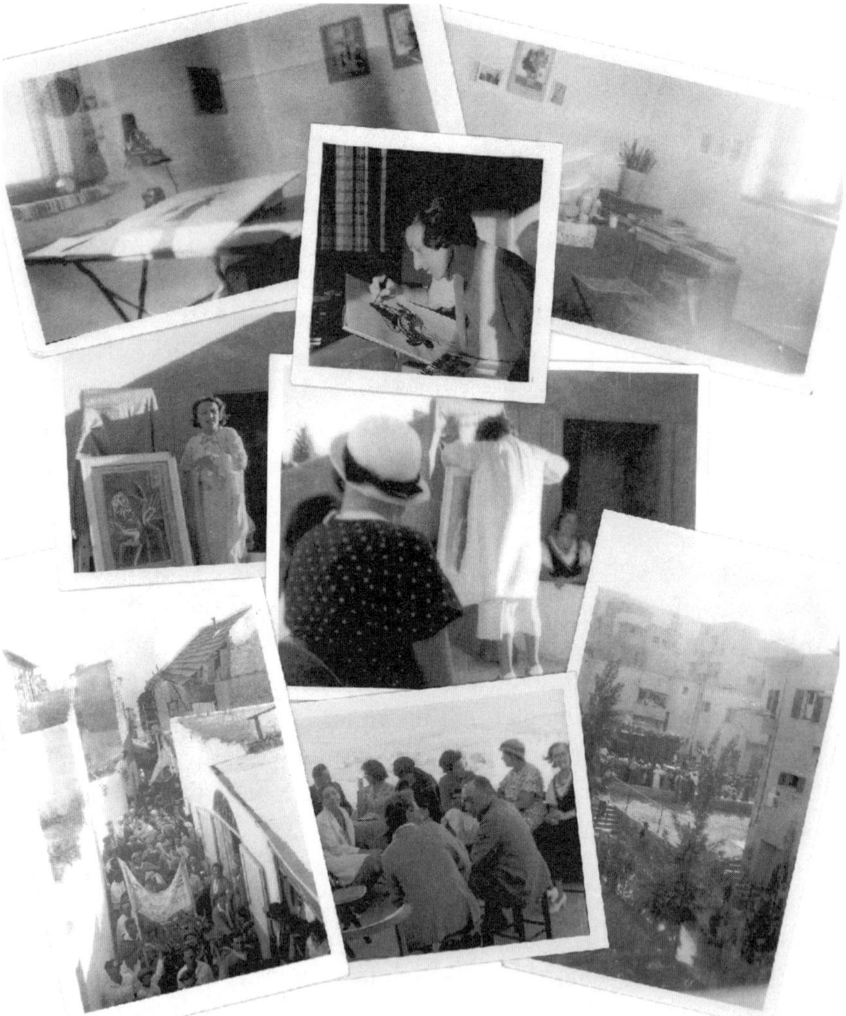

did not take long before all the Jewish women were wearing wigs, not white, but black and brown as you see them to this day. Maybe this is just a story, but we do know for certain that orthodox women must cover their hair for fear of arousing in men some strange, irresistible feelings.

Back on my roof, the audience had arrived very punctually. After being served a cool, refreshing drink, everybody sat down and I put one picture up on the easel and began to talk. It was truly wonderful. There were questions, comments, discussion and even arguments. They were curious about my style and a lively debate ensued as to the merits of the abstract or semi-abstract approach versus the representational one. To cover all the paintings and drawings at that rate took more than three hours. Suddenly, it was twilight. It seems that there is very little sunset time in Israel as compared with the length and intensity of our sunsets in the United States. To everyone s delight a full moon appeared in the deep, ultramarine blue sky. We turned on some music, drank juice, tea, and nibbled on nuts and fruits while others danced. That was an exhibition not soon to be forgotten. There were reports in newspapers and magazines, and the discussions continued the following weekend.

Then the time came for packing much more luggage than I had brought with me, and for saying goodbye to the many friends I had made. A couple of puppeteers, wonderful friends, gave me a delightful little hand puppet as a farewell gift. This little puppet I named "Spunky" made many friends for me on the boat. Spunky sat in a small, hand embroidered shoulder bag and became the center of attention wherever I went. I was always followed by a group of delighted children with whom the little puppet carried on conversations and sang many of the songs I had learned in my first great experience in the land of my ancient ancestors.

CHAPTER 8 – HOMEWARD VIA ENGLAND

My next stop was going to be London. But I planned to spend a few days in Paris to say "hello" to some of my friends, make another visit to the Louvre and some of the galleries. It was pleasant, too, to sit in an out-of-door cafe with a friend drinking an aperitif or a "chocolat", watching the endless stream of humanity passing by. Parisians loved to spend the long summer evenings in the cafes with their friends, eating, drinking, chatting, laughing.

Another reason for stopping off in Paris was to pick up mail at the American Express where all American tourists came to receive letters from home and to send letters back. It was also a popular rendezvous for Americans as well as others. Among my letters was one from my sister Ettie, in which she told me to write to a young woman in London. Her name was Rae Braham. I had met her a few years earlier when she came to America to visit her cousin May, Ettie's friend. I wrote to Rae immediately and told her that I was planning to be in London the following week and might I call upon her. That was on Tuesday. On Thursday I received a frantic note:

"Dear Temima, Don't wait until next week. Come immediately! Seven of us, four boys and three girls, have chartered a boat for a week to sail along the Norfolk Broads and we need one more girl. We are leaving Friday afternoon. Please come immediately. We need you and I promise you a wonderful time."

Well, I was not going to miss such an opportunity. Imagine, spending a whole week on a boat with seven young people, listening to the King's English, sailing all day and mooring up at night at quaint villages, which were celebrating summer's end with fairs and festivals. So, the next morning, Friday, found me crossing the English Channel, full of anticipation. And I was not disappointed. My English hosts immediately adopted me as one of them. It was a week of fun and new experiences. To sail along on the Broads in full sunlight waving to passing boats filled with other vacationing sailors like us was pure joy. I listened to their singing of all sorts of wonderful English ballads and popular songs I had never heard before, humming along during the verse and then joining them in the chorus.

We moored up one night at Yarmouth, a colorful village, filled with the excitement of a country fair. The sounds, the smells were intoxicating. We ate the famous Yarmouth kippered herrings, a taste I shall never forget. It brought back memories of winter mornings in Brownsville when, occasionally, my father would come home with a kipper that he had bought in the market. He prepared it, filling the room with the smell of fresh, fried, smoked fish. The taste was very different from the familiar gefilte fish to which we were so accustomed. My father had spent enough time in London while the family was still in Pinsk to acquire something of a British accent and he carried the broad "a" with him to the grave. He had never told us about his stay in London. It has always been a mystery to me and I m sorry to say that I never learned anymore about it.

On our return to London, Rae refused to let me go to a hotel. When I met her parents, hardworking yet most generous in their hospitality, they insisted on my spending my last three weeks in England in their home. Imagine being awakened every morning by her mother, "Mummy," a little lady who would not permit me to get out of bed before having the most wonderful tea and delicious, hot buns or scones. Rae's father took time off from running his tobacconist shop to show me the wonders of London, and when Rae returned from work, she took over the duties of tour guide.

Rae also introduced me to Archie, a good friend, and supplied us with theatre tickets to see a play *"Tempest in a Teapot*!" The theatre manager asked us to play a small part in the play. We readily accepted. We were quite an attractive couple. We were both sun burnt and dressed in brilliant summer colors. Archie wore a bright pink shirt, open at the collar. I wore a chartreuse suit. Together, we looked as though the theatre had dressed us for our part in the play. The action took place in a courtroom. The two of us sat in the center of the first row of the jury box. We were told to act naturally, as we would if we were bona fide members of a jury. "Just listen and react normally", we were told. The theatre darkened, the curtains parted and the show started. For a few moments, I felt nervous with butterflies in my stomach. Soon, however, I became so interested in the play that I forgot that I was playing a part. During a tense moment in the courtroom scene, a shot was fired. Startled, I jumped up spontaneously and cried, "Oh my!" I was later congratulated by the manager for my convincing performance.

I spent many hours in the British Museum, a storehouse of treasures from all over the world, especially from Egypt. The paintings at the Tate National Gallery brought back memories of wonderful art history lectures in art school with Howard Giles and Emil Bisttram. Seeing the originals was like meeting old friends.

Soon it was "goodbye" again, with many mixed emotions.

CHAPTER 9 – NEW OPPORTUNITIES

After a few days on the elegant Queen Mary, I returned to home and family and immediate job hunting. The real excitement was in preparing to show my work. That meant having frames made, (no inexpensive undertaking even in those days), finding a gallery willing to show the work of an unknown, and picking up the threads of my life again.

I heard that many artists had succeeded in getting jobs with the WPA painting murals for public institutions like post offices, public libraries, courthouses and others. I wanted to paint murals, too. So, I applied for a job, filled out a lengthy application form and had an interview. All went well until I was asked, "Does any member of your family have a job?" When they heard that my sister Ettie was working, I was told even though I was well qualified, that jobs were to be given to artists who were the sole support of their family. I did learn later that many artists had not answered all the questions completely truthfully.

Apparently, fate had other plans for me. The exhibition at the Delphic Studios, a gallery on Fifth Avenue, turned out to be very well received. In the hall next to my show was another exhibition, the work of Orozco, a well-known Mexican mural painter whose work I admired immensely.

My first exhibition was followed by others. I rented a loft on West 56th Street and began to teach children and adult art classes. It was a very comfortable and well appointed studio, born out of a dreary apartment with the help and expert carpentry ability of my uncle, Yuda Meir Cohen, my mother's brother. We worked out a very compact arrangement of an easel, which could be raised or lowered, folded flat against the wall, or turned into a table. It was very convenient for me because it left lots of open space for movement.

I loved my uncle and he adored me. Whenever he came to visit my mother, he would wait for me to come home so that we could have one of our long discussions. Generally, we spoke about some subject from the bible. Yude-Meir enjoyed talking with me because he could quote from the commentators on the bible, like Rashi and Unkulus, and know that I would understand. Because he was quite a scholar, I enjoyed him as well.

In my studio I had many interesting experiences with my students. Teaching children who came to art class because they loved to is a delight for both student and teacher. However, when you can be responsible for a more hopeful outlook on life on the part of someone who seemed to have no future, that is truly a rewarding experience.

This is what happened. I was lecturing to a group of women about my paintings, which were on exhibition. I presented many ideas during that lecture. One idea, on which I had laid special emphasis, was my basic belief that all people are potentially creators. This seemed to make a strong impression on one young woman in the audience. She came up to me after the talk.

"Do you really believe that everyone can paint - can create - can make things? Do you think that I can do something with my life in this field? There has been nothing for me since my husband s death."

She was a young widow, desperate, with two little children dependent on her alone. For them she had to live although the desire to live, was not there. For months now she had felt like an automaton, doing those things which had to be done, for the sake of the children. For her there was nothing - until I threw out the challenge that stirred a chord within her.

She came to my studio the next day. I gave her something simple, something to relax her inner tension - in a medium that was soothing to the touch and good for the spirit - finger painting. Fingers glide over the smooth, wet surface with the ease and grace of a skilled skater on the ice. It is fun! There was no need for planning, arranging, solving serious problems. One look at my busy new student and I saw that the block of ice inside was slowly beginning to thaw. Her eyes were sparkling, her cheeks flushed, her hair tossing - all signs of new life. When the session was over, she asked to take the paintings home to show her boys.

On the way home, she later told me, she stopped off at the grocer s to shop for supper. While waiting her turn, she noticed the grocer remove the round, clean cover from a fresh butter tub. (Those were the days). Then, an idea! "May I have that cover?" After supper the butter-tub cover went through a metamorphosis. She trimmed her finger paintings to size and fitted and pasted them on the cover, top and bottom. She found some colorful leatherette and deftly twisted it around the circular edge. The cover became a decorative tray, taking its place very graciously on the mantelpiece. Soon, all her friends wanted trays. Their department store wanted to sell them. Things were really beginning to hum.

I noticed that no matter what medium we worked with in the studio, she made use of that medium in some practical way. After she learned to use clay, she bought a tubful for her boys and later formed a clay modeling class, with them and their friends as the core.

When, however, I gave her first lesson in metal work, I realized that this was her medium. Her fingers handled the copper with confidence and authority. She seemed to know exactly what the metal needed. She twisted and turned it with dexterity, deftness and with particularly loving care. Observing the expression on her face and the ease with which she handled the material, I knew that this was the field in which she could find fulfillment.

From me she went on to study jewelry-making in a school which specialized in this craft. Months later she invited me to her home. Her dining room had been transformed into a showroom. Here she displayed the jewelry, trays and other silver objects that she had made in her little workshop, converted from a large closet in her apartment. More time passed. Then I heard that she had opened a silvercraft shop on one of the more fashionable parts of the city. Five craftsmen worked for her. Business was really growing. What a change in her life!

CHAPTER 10 – THE SYNAGOGUE MURAL

Now, things began to move quickly for me. Apparently, there was a good reason for my not getting a job at the WPA. There were other plans for me. In 1935, Dr. Mordecai Kaplan, who was the Dean of the Teachers Institute at the Jewish Theological Seminary, and who had been my teacher of religion there, called me into his office and offered me a job to teach art at the Institute. His daughter Judith was to teach Music. What a wonderful opportunity to introduce the arts, into an area from which the students were heretofore excluded. I had many fascinating experiences teaching there.

Then Dr. Kaplan asked me to paint a mural for his synagogue at the S.A.J. (The Society for the Advancement of Judaism at 15 West 86 Street in Manhattan.) What an opportunity! What a challenge! Since I had recently been through my first thrilling Israel experience, the mural was to be an expression of that experience.

After Dr. Kaplan and a committee of the board of directors had accepted the sketches, I shut myself away from the world in my studio, and began to work on the mural. It was to be placed on the rear wall of the synagogue over the large entrance doors, covering an area of about 200 square feet. It would be painted with oil on canvas. I worked feverishly, in my studio, non-stop, day and night with an excitement I had never experienced before.

The theme of the mural was "Old and New Elements in Palestine." One panel dealt with the ancient architecture, Hassidim praying, Hassidim dancing, young children studying in the old *heder* set-up, money-lenders and the many colorful types of characters walking through the narrow, arched, cobble stone streets of Old Jerusalem. Another panel dealt with the new land - new architecture, students at the Hebrew University, scientists, researchers, the Haifa Technion, youths marching and workers involved in construction. The long center panel covered the many varied activities of a kibbutz during the harvesting of the citrus fruits.

About eighty human figures filled the large space, a fact which was to eventually provoke the wrath of those who still strictly followed the ancient interpretation of the commandment, *"Thou shalt not make unto thee graven images."* In the Third Century AD, the walls of the Synagogue at Dura-Europas were covered frescoes covered with over-life-size figures from the Bible. Since then, however, the literal interpretation of the Bible had been strictly enforced.

My mother was there the evening that the unveiling of the mural was to take place. The S.A.J. Synagogue was filled to capacity. Cloth curtains covered the mural. I really don't remember all the speeches. I was much too excited to remember anything except that Dr. Kaplan spoke warmly and with spirit about the importance of art in the life of a nation, and of all human beings. The most wonderful thing that happened was the change in my mother's attitude toward my art. She had never really understood the strength of my obsession with art. But my mother understood Dr. Kaplan's

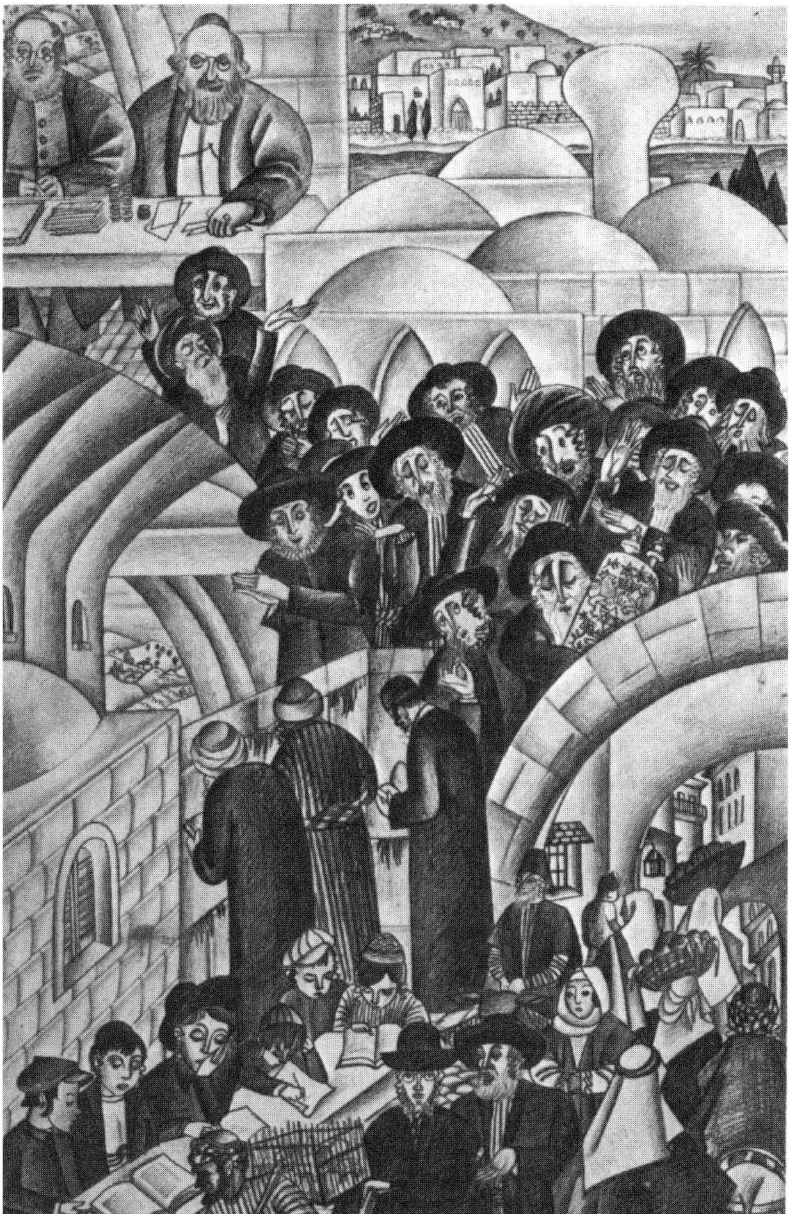

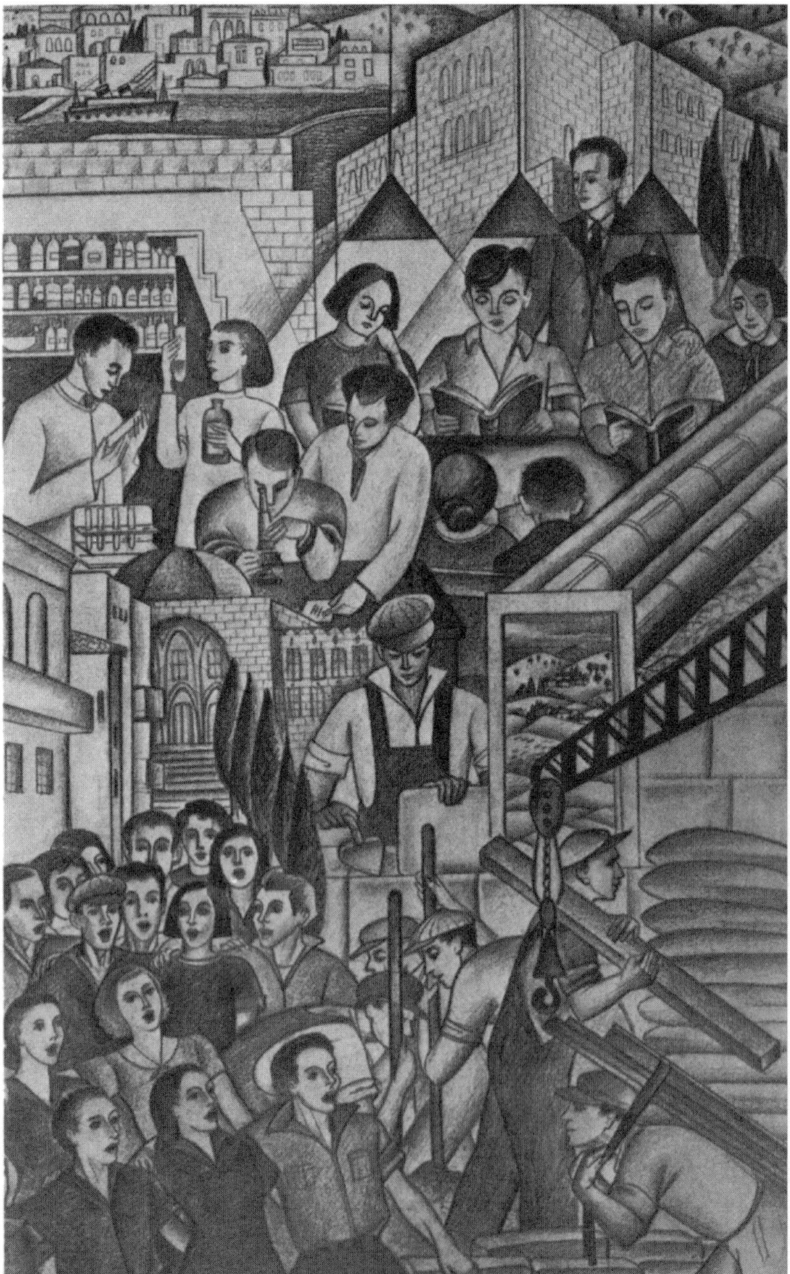

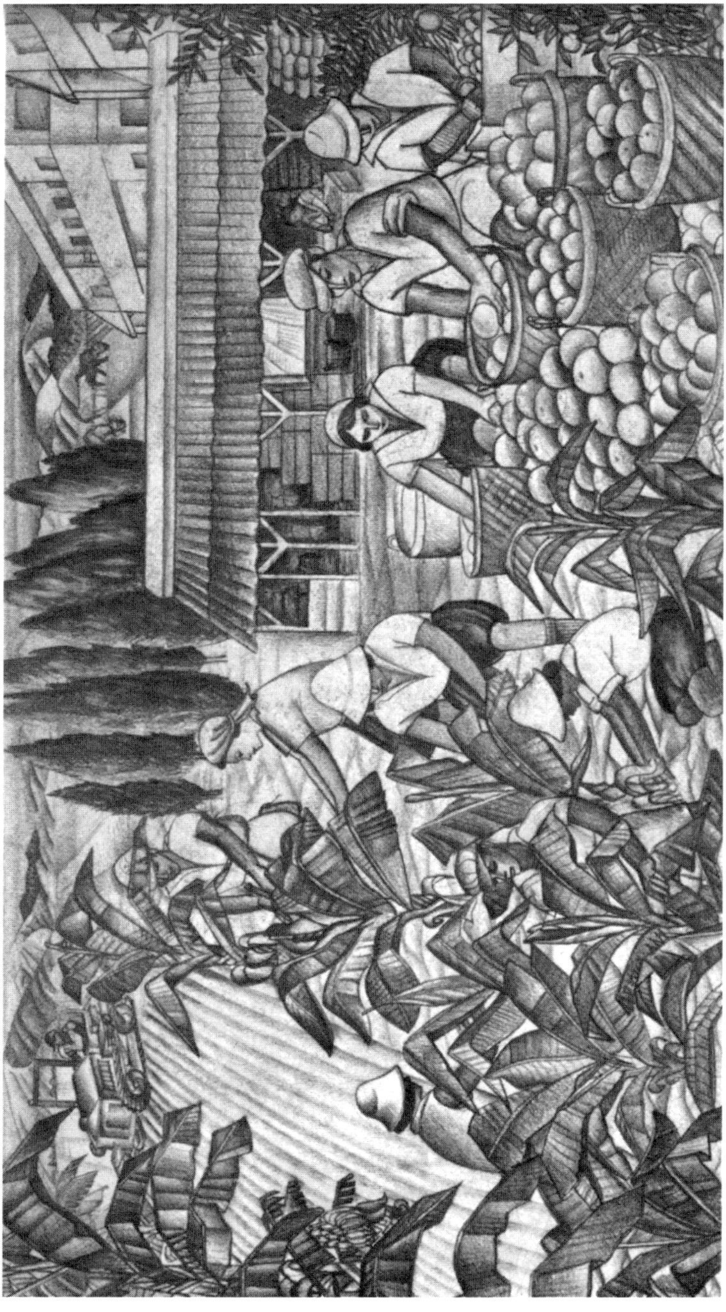

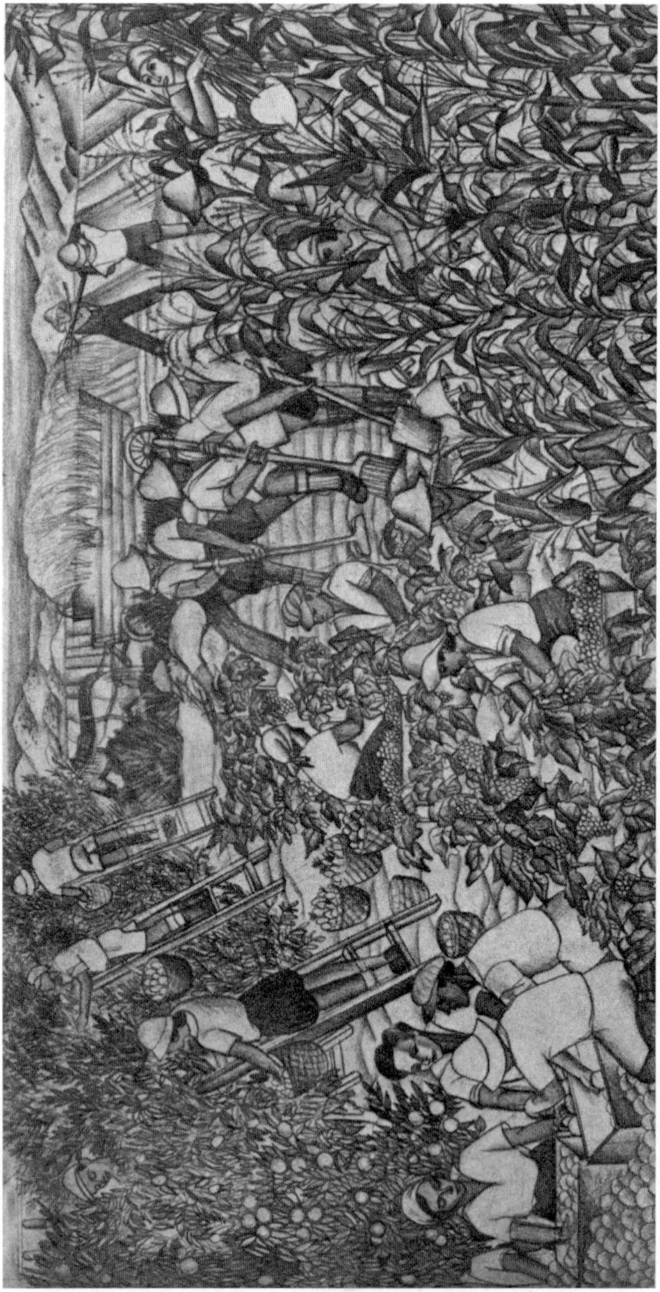

meaning when the whole congregation gasped in excitement as the curtains were opened and the mural was revealed. From that time on she never again questioned my passion for art.

As it turned out, when news of the mural project spread there were many people who were impressed by the creative thought and courage involved in the reintroduction of figures into synagogue decoration. Letters and newspaper clippings came pouring in from all over the world in all languages. Photographs of the mural were reproduced in magazines. I remember one magazine that arrived from Hungary with a double page spread of reproductions of the mural and many columns of text in a language that neither I nor anybody else that I knew, could understand then or now. It was a most exciting time in my life.

CHAPTER 11 – ANOTHER MURAL PROJECT

A short time later in 1935, Dr. Albert Schoolman, the founder and director of Camp Cejwin, asked me to paint a mural overlooking the pulpit area of the camp synagogue. I was delighted to have been commissioned to paint this mural because I felt very close to the camp and its philosophy. I had served as counselor of a bunk of darling little girls and as art counselor for several seasons. Now after many years, I would be returning to camp as a mural painter.

I remember that my first year as regular counselor was a tremendous learning experience for me. I threw myself into the job with all my energy and fervor. Besides my expected duties in charge of a group of seven year olds, I also taught Hebrew classes, led morning services and Sabbath services and assisted in the arts and crafts program. I worked a lot and learned a lot and loved every minute of it.

After the first few days in camp, the routine more or less crystallized. It was very easy to form the habit of going for a swim before lunch, or of spending an hour in the arts and crafts bunk, or at nature study, dramatics, dance or music. But one could not ever seem to get used to the idea of jumping out of a warm bed on a chilly morning for calisthenics. It was hard at a command, to send one s arms into the cold air away from the still warm body.

Then there was the short morning religious service, which took place just before breakfast. Because of its proximity to the meal hour, services were held near the mess hall, so that while we were supposed to be preoccupied with spiritual thoughts, the delicious smells of hot cocoa, flavorful coffee, buttered toast and scrambled eggs mixed with the clatter of dishes and rattle of silverware, all joined to tease and taunt us to the point where we could think of nothing else but our empty stomachs.

The service itself, unfortunately, offered no competition to the appealing distraction of the forthcoming breakfast. It was meaningless and uninspired. Many words were read in a language strange to one s ears. English translations, being literal, shed no light on concepts that seemed too far removed from children s understanding. Yet children have deep religious feelings. So I decided to take a mixed group of twelve-year-olds on an overnight hike. This was my regular painting group, so that the children knew me quite well and felt secure with me as we climbed to the top of a neighboring hill and chose a site for our night s adventure.

Summit Mountain afforded us broad horizons beyond our limited vision. We prepared our camp for the night, unpacking our supplies, building a fire, toasting marshmallows and singing jolly camp songs and then old, familiar ones. Then, by the light of the glowing embers, we crept into our sleeping bags. After some stories, some funny, some spooky, silence fell. The children lay on their backs looking at a sky full of stars. There was the Big Dipper, the North Star, Venus, Orion, the Hunter, and millions of others. Then came an awareness of night noises, locusts, crickets, the rustle of leaves as a slight breeze played through the trees. Then sleep, and a great stillness.

At dawn, the children began to awake one by one, but without communicating with one another. They seemed to feel part of a profoundly stirring experience, which, though shared by all, was yet extremely personal and private. Soft, warm tints began to creep into the cool blue sky. The last stars began to fade away . Birds began to move around, their song soft and muted. There is a feeling as of an orchestra tuning up before the playing of the overture. It became lighter. The color began to echo the brilliance of the gold, rose and crimson of yesterday s sunset. Roosters crowed as the sun rose in a burst of glory behind the rim of Mount Summit and lit up every blade of grass with a dewy halo. Now the campers are sitting up as if drawn out of themselves by something much greater than any of them. Day has arrived, the spell broken. Only twelve years old- but at certain moments during the night they felt as old as the universe.

I knew that as a result of their experience, these boys and girls would understand the meaning of prayer. So, at our next painting lesson, I asked them to talk about their experience on the mountain, or paint it, dance it, sing it, or use any other means they wished to express their ideas. The results were most impressive. They wrote poems and prose, worked out in rhythms the sequence from night and darkness to light and day. They wrote a playlet, which took place on the stars and painted the most sensitive paintings, many of them in the free strokes of finger paint and abstraction. We read the poems. "Why, these sound like prayers, but easier to understand." The results of the expression of their deep feelings became the basis for the next morning service. The last few services at camp did not have to compete with the aroma of cocoa and scrambled eggs. There was a richer flavor in the singing, dancing and poetry of the children who, for the first time, were conscious of a unity of spirit between the ancient bards and themselves. Together they sang "Hallelujah" and understood what the prayer meant.

Every Friday was hike day in camp. The campers marched away with knapsacks on their backs singing camp songs lustily and looking forward to an exciting day of hiking, playing games and eating lots of different kinds of food around a campfire. With campers away, maintenance crews attacked the bunks, removing the cots, scrubbing the floors and preparing the camp for the advent of the Sabbath. On the return of the campers, there was a rush to the lake for a quick swim followed by showers, hair shampoos and special dressup for Sabbath services followed by a sumptuous Shabbat dinner.

I introduced another idea for Friday hike day. Any camper who preferred a day of art instead of a hike could join me with pad, paper and watercolors to go away from camp to paint directly from nature. It was great fun and when we returned glowing from a day of pleasure and accomplishment, we hung up our paintings to share our work with the other campers and to enjoy their appreciation.

Against this backdrop very favorable camp experiences, and wonderful memories, I was now asked to paint a mural. This was to be my very own personal experience and I was jubilant. To spend long summer days painting in the spacious boathouse right on the lake with wonderful light, fresh, sweet air and surrounded on all sides by beautiful trees and bushes. What more could an artist ask for? One beautiful day followed after another. Working was pure joy. At the end of the day, there was always progress.

Occasionally, Dr. Schoolman would stop by for a break from his responsibilities as Camp Director. One day he told me that he was having a very serious problem with a group of fifteen, fifteen-year-olds. These boys refused to attend Hebrew studies. They disliked the classroom tent in hot summer. They were not interested in learning the letters of the Hebrew alphabet. The teacher was not inspiring. The whole situation was very boring.

The boys revolted. Instead of attending class, they ran off to the baseball diamond. This was, of course, a sign of imminent disaster because - what does a younger child want more than anything else, than to be or to emulate a fifteen-year-old. How long would it be before other kids ran off to the baseball field as a substitute for Hebrew studies. At the pleading) of Dr. Schoolman, whom I admired very much, I agreed to take over those rebellious boys as a challenge. So now, I had to divide my time between painting the mural and working with those fifteen-fifteen year-olds.

I met with the boys that first day at the lake s edge as far away from their former study tent as possible. After introducing myself, I said, " I understand that you are great baseball players. Would you believe that the only time I went to a baseball game was when I was in the third grade. Because I had been on the honor roll for the whole term, I was given a ticket to a baseball game in Ebbet s Field in Brooklyn." I proceeded then to relate this exciting first (and last) baseball experience. I was only seven years old and could not understand why those "big men" kept swinging a stick, dropping it and running around to the shouts and screams of the crowd. Soon it was over and I was still waiting for the show to start. My new students were much amused and agreed to teach me the game, then and there. So, off we went to the baseball diamond. However, we never got there.

As we walked, I told them that I had very limited sports experience since all my time was devoted to art. Yet, during my recent trip to Israel, I was very impressed with a soccer game played with such amazing skill by the Maccabee team and I enjoyed it as much as if it had been a magnificent dance recital. T"hey play soccer in Israel?!" exclaimed one youngster, "I thought old folks go there to die!" At that, we sat down and I began to relate some of my most exciting adventures.

Then began a fascinating project, both for the boys and me. Let it suffice to say that the summer ended on a high pitch of excitement for my students. A whole assembly was devoted to the fifteen-year-olds presentation of their summer s work, which consisted of a study of the people, geography, occupations, forms of transportation, ancient and modern sites and institutions in the land. All was done in three dimensional maps, models, dioramas using every conceivable material including wood, clay, plaster, metal, balsa wood, paint. They presented their work with pride and confidence. "Now", I said to Dr. Schoolman, "is the time for the boys to resume their Hebrew studies, because now they are fully motivated."

Meanwhile, work on my mural was proceeding well. The subject I had chosen was "Shevuot Harvest Festival" featuring a parade of children carrying baskets of the first fruits of the harvest as well as sheaves of wheat and garlands of flowers. Older boys and girls carry flags while a little child leads a little lamb. All takes place in front of landscape of the hills and trees of Haifa.

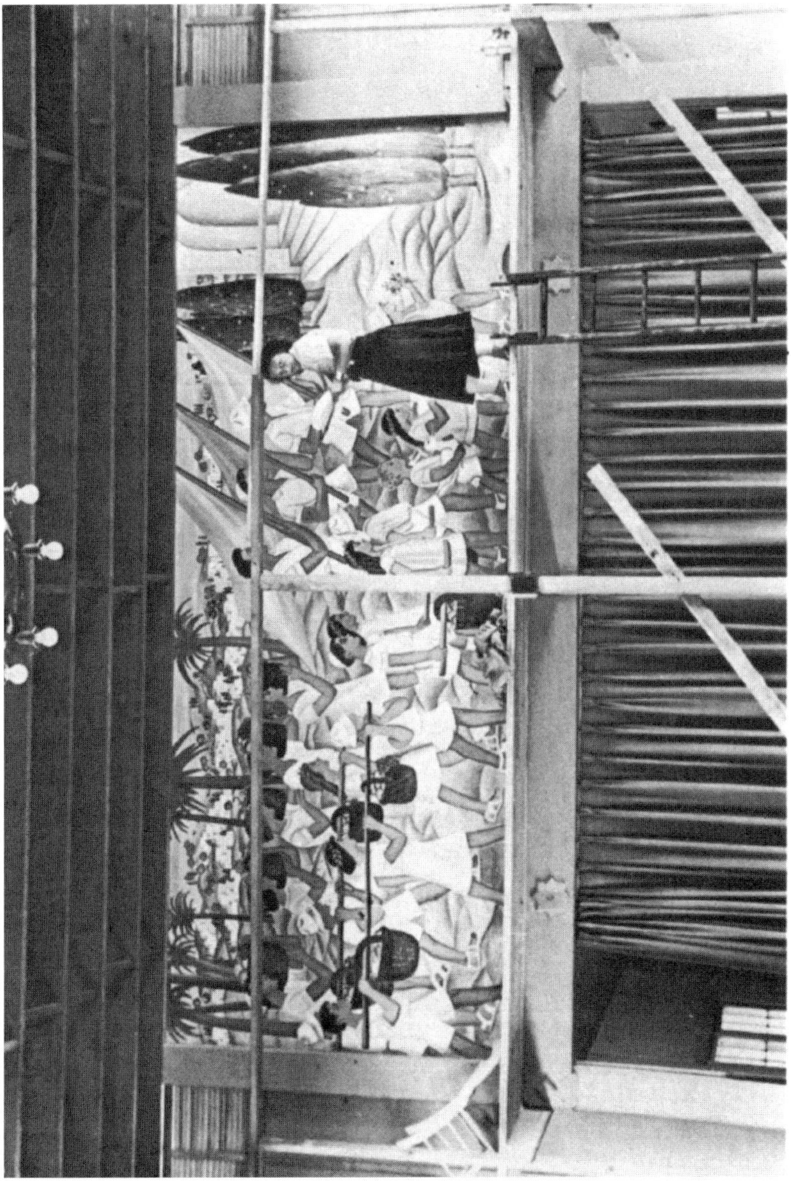

CHAPTER 12 – RESTORATION

Fifty years later, I received a call from Camp Cejwin. "For fifty years", the voice said, "campers have been sitting at services with their eyes glued to your mural. Now it needs to be restored." Hot summers, freezing winters, high humidity and a leaky roof had all taken their toll. "Since we would like to celebrate the mural s golden anniversary, we should like to have it restored. Can you suggest somebody to do the job?"

My answer was simple, "No one restores that mural but I!" So, a few days later, I arrived at Camp Cejwin, fifty years after that memorable summer when the mural had been set in place with much pomp and ceremony. The camp was different now. The old girl s side on the hill had been sold. Now, the camp housed bungalows for both boys and girls.

A sixteen-foot scaffold had been erected according to my directions. On it were all the materials I had ordered - Winston and Newton oil paints, brushes, turpentine, some clean rags and a stool. As I began to climb the tall ladder, somebody began climbing behind me. Looking back I saw this nice young man right behind me. "Where are you going?" I asked. "Well, I'm following you just in case," he answered. True, I then already eighty years old, an age at which one is not expected to climb sixteen-foot ladders. But, I said to him, "You don t have to worry about me. I have spent more time on ladders in my work than on the ground. So, get off the ladder, sit down and watch me work".

By this time a number of people had gathered to see how I would go about with the restoration. One person joined me on the scaffold, the arts and crafts councilor, who wanted to learn the process. I was delighted to have her help me because I had only a day and a half to finish the job. She was a lovely young woman and we worked together very well.

The first thing I did, to everybody s amazement, was to pick up a wide brush and with strong strokes, rubbed down the entire surface of the painting, causing a shower of flakes to fall down and cover the floor below. Gasps of horror filled the room. "Don t worry," I assured them, "these are loose paint flakes dried out by time and the weather. Now I can start painting and bringing the mural back to life."

All day long, campers of all ages came to the large hall to watch me paint. They were fascinated and asked questions which I delighted to answer from my high perch on the scaffold. Several teenage girls who were studying art in school spent hours on end watching the progress and asking very intelligent questions. The next morning, my helper and I were both on the scaffold at six o clock in the morning. The goal I had set for myself was to complete the restoration before six p.m., so that the Friday evening service would continue as in the past. At a quarter before six, I climbed down the ladder, looked up at the mural and was satisfied that it looked as fresh and beautiful as on the day it was completed fifty years before.

CHAPTER 13 – RETURN TO KIBBUTZ

In 1936 I was asked to show my paintings at the annual convention of the Hadassah Organization. The convention took place at the Willard Hotel in Washington. It was a most prestigious hotel. The exhibition was displayed in a large hall and was very well attended.

One afternoon a young man came to see the show. He had come from Israel on Kibbutz business. His name was Moshe Furmansky. We spent a long time discussing my work and then he said something, which was forever to change my life. He said, "Would you like to come and spend some time in our Kibbutz? We work very hard in the kibbutz. By 4 a.m., we are at work in the fields, in the barns, in the kitchen, in the chicken coops, in the tree nurseries and in every other area of work. At the end of the day, we are so weary that we cannot go to the city to enjoy exhibitions of art. It would be wonderful to have a young artist living and painting in the kibbutz and sharing with us ideas about art. We hear names like Picasso, and Matisse, but we don't know anything about them. And wouldn't it be great for our children to learn about them, too? Would you come and teach us something about the new trends in art? What do you say, will you come?"

He was asking me to be artist-in-residence, a concept that is very familiar now but was completely unheard of then. I was very much interested in living in a kibbutz since, during my stay in Jerusalem in 1934 I had visited kibbutzim, but had not lived in one for any length of time. I answered him as follows, "Moshe, you are a very nice young man. But I don t know you from Adam. I'd gladly come to your kibbutz, and I will, but only if I receive an invitation from the kibbutz." Three weeks later, a letter arrived from Kibbutz Mishmar Haemek, graciously inviting me to come to the kibbutz and stay there as long as I wished to.

I started packing immediately. Before I left, some Hadassah women asked me to do a film for them on the subject of Youth Aliyah, showing how the children saved from the clutches of the Nazis in Europe were adjusting to their new life in Israel. Despite my protests of having no experience in film making, they loaded me up with reels of film and a Kodak motion picture camera saying, "You can do it. You are an artist. You can do anything." This was a challenge I could not refuse. So I left for my next adventure with a trunk full of art supplies, topped off with a layer of yellow boxes of Kodak motion picture film.

When the boat anchored at Alexandria, Egypt, I received a cable from my parents, which urged me to return to the United States: "There are Arab riots in Palestine, return immediately." Of course, I would not turn back. I was safe, I assured myself. I was going to a kibbutz. A few days later, we arrived in Haifa. The transatlantic liner was too large to enter the port and had to drop anchor in deeper waters. From there, tenders would transport the passengers and luggage into Haifa Port. Before we disembarked, we were warned to be extremely careful not to irritate the Arab customs officials who were going to examine our baggage.

When my turn came to be inspected, I opened my trunk and there right on top was a full layer of containers of moving picture film. The customs inspector, a fat Arab dressed in an abayah and a fez, picked up one container, looked at it, then at me, and asked, "Film?" If I agreed with him, one of two things would undoubtedly happen - either the film would be confiscated or I would have to pay an exorbitant custom tax - neither of which I was not ready to face. So, out of the air I picked my answer. "No," I countered, "Cinema!" "Film," he insisted. "No, cinema!," was my response. Film! Cinema! Film! Cinema! Bystanders were obviously nervous. How long would this go on? And, what next? To everybody s relief, however, the inspector suddenly dropped the film into the trunk, slammed the cover closed, scribbled an "X" in white chalk and went on to the next person on line, muttering under his breath.

In Haifa, I called the kibbutz. I was told to go to a hotel and wait until I received a call. Apparently, the kibbutz bus schedule had been disrupted by the riots. The Arabs, knowing that the bus left Kibbutz Mishmar Haemek for Haifa at certain specified hours, lay in wait for it, shooting, throwing stones and breaking windows. Therefore, the kibbutz changed the schedule, going at irregular times or skipping certain days altogether. They recommended a small hotel in which I could wait for them to send the bus.

The next day, they called and told me to meet the bus at a certain corner in Haifa at four o'clock in the afternoon. The bus arrived on time. It was crowded and the driver apologetically offered me a seat next to him, a five-gallon can on which he had placed a little cushion. I was delighted and accepted immediately. What could be better than to sit next to the driver, Dodiah, with eyes so deeply blue they seemed to be spilling over onto his eyelashes, and have him describe and explain everything?

My pleasure at sitting next to was spoiled by a young man who came from the rear and said in Hebrew, "Let the young lady take my seat and I will sit on the can." "Oh, no, that s not necessary," I said, "I would prefer sitting here." However, he insisted politely and I noticed that the passengers were becoming restless. I did not want to add to their nervousness, so I reluctantly went to the back of the bus and the young man sat down in my coveted seat. In my frustration I vowed that I would never to speak to that fellow again. "That fellow" was Zvi, the man I was to marry.

We arrived in the Kibbutz without mishap and I was briefed as to how to manage during an Arab attack, which would undoubtedly occur that night as it did every night. If, at night, I heard a gunshot in the courtyard, I must realize that an attack was in progress. I was to get dressed in dark clothes and run bent over and in a zigzag line to the shelter, which was in the basement in the children s house and school. There were only two concrete structures in the Kibbutz at that time, the school and the small building that housed the Steinway grand piano that was sent as a gift from America.

Sure enough, that night the inevitable attack came. I ran in the darkness toward the shelter. The distance was only about 100 feet but, to me, it seemed

Kibbutz Mishmar Haemek

Kibbutz Life

Temima at Mishmar Haemek - 1934

like 100 miles. Now I was in the basement shelter. It was dark except for thin slits of red light, which flashed through the closed shutters. The Arabs had set fire to the forest. The shelter was filled with people. They were so silent that the only audible sound was their breathing. I was certain that everyone could hear my heart beating. I was petrified. When had my life in such jeopardy?

As I waited in the darkness in that sad assemblage, I could only feel my panic. Would there be a tomorrow? Suddenly, I felt somebody tapping me on the shoulder and a man s voice said, "Temima, I am a teacher in the school. Would you lecture to my class tomorrow morning on Greek Art?" At that moment all fear left me. Is there a tomorrow? Yes!

In a short time, we could hear trucks going up to the forest to drive away the arsonists, put out the fires. The forest was very precious to the kibbutz. They had worked so hard to plant a forest where only rocks and brambles had been before. Because of their untiring effort it was transformed to a flourishing forest. They finally had beautiful shade trees, which started with a road lined with trees leading up to the "*chorshah*" (forest) where, every Shabbat, parents and children made a pilgrimage to see the trees and how they were growing. Now it was being burned every night. But each time the *chaverim* drove off the marauders, cleared away the burnt timbers, refreshed the soil, and planted new saplings.

Chaverim on Kibbutz

CHAPTER 14 – THE KIBUTZNIKS

Life in the Kibbutz fascinated me. Most of the members had come from Russia and Poland. They were, for the most part, professionals - writers, lawyers, scholars in many fields, actors, artists, musicians, engineers - in a word, the Jewish "intelligentzia". These same brilliant people were now clearing land of large boulders, digging ditches, working in construction, shoveling manure, driving tractors, cooking, scrubbing pots, etc. etc., etc.

Mordecai Bentov was one of the founders of Kibbutz Mishmar Haemek. He was also one of the signers of the Proclamation of the Establishment of the State of Israel in 1948. He was in the cabinet as the Minister of Reconstruction and spent most of the week carrying on his duties in the Knesset in Jerusalem. However, he returned to the Kibbutz for Shabbat. There he carried on his duties as a member of the Kibbutz. He prided himself on the fact that nobody could scrub pots as thoroughly as he. Cleaning the kitchen was his job and he performed it with as much care and diligence as when he wrote a column for a newspaper or prepared a speech for the Knesset.

Once, a delegation from Guiana arrived in Jerusalem to seek advice from the Minister of Reconstruction. Upon learning that Bentov was home in his Kibbutz, they drove to Mishmar Haemek. When they inquired for Minister Bentov, they were directed to the kitchen. There stood the Minister of Reconstruction, at the sink scrubbing away at one of many huge pots big enough to hold soup for several hundred people.

I had heard of another occasion when the brother of one of the members came from America to visit him. The American was dismayed upon finding his brother in the barn shoveling manure. "Is this what you are doing here!" he exclaimed, "You were a Professor of Literature in one of the most prestigious universities in Europe, and this is what you have chosen instead!" The brother put down his shovel and said, "Dear brother, I have found a new life for myself, helping to build a homeland for my people, where we can live free and with dignity. I have never been so happy in my life."

One of my favorite people was Meta. Meta had been an actress in Europe. The first time I met her was probably the second or third day of my arrival in the Kibbutz. There she stood dressed in white overalls, a worker's cap holding back her curly black hair. She had laughing blue eyes, a lively, smiling face covered with a delicate sprinkling of plaster of Paris, even her eyelashes. For Meta was the kibbutz plasterer. Whenever plastering had to be done whether in Mishmar Haemek or in any other kibbutz, the call went out for Meta. She, the creative actress, was also the best plasterer and was constantly in demand.

I learned later that she had also organized an actor's troupe, wrote and produced plays, directed and acted in them, and arranged for the Kibbutz actors to perform at other kibbutzim, towns and cities. She also wrote and produced scripts for the radio program "Jerusalem Calling." In later years, Meta prepared elaborate pageants on Jewish History for the State of Israel.

Meta

On one of my later visits, I was fortunate to attend the famous Dance Festival in Kibbutz Dalia. I shall never forget that night. The deep blue sky was rich with stars. The audience sat in tiers on a hillside. On the opposite hill, the dancing took place. Every kibbutz created its own dance. A kibbutz that had developed a fishing industry did a fisherman s dance with nets. Kibbutz Dalia did a fathers and sons dance, and so on. Then, out of the dark mountain came a group of Arabs dancing the well-known *debka* circle dance. Then darkness and suddenly on the other side of the mountain, a light, and a group of Jews emerged dancing the same debka. Then darkness and again a large spotlight played on a large group of Arabs and Jews dancing the debka, together, to the thunderous applause and approving shouts of the audience. When I looked through the festival program, I noticed that the organizer, director and producer of this amazingly inspired event was Meta, from Kibbutz Mishmar Haemek, and I was proud.

Another person I was very fond of was Elisheva, a young lawyer from Berlin. She was strikingly beautiful with long dark hair pulled tightly back from a finely chiseled face. She was slight and slim, like a gazelle. Elisheva had been a lawyer in Berlin, but she left and joined the Kibbutz doing menial labor in the laundry or the kitchen, scrubbing, mopping and everything that had to be done.

Once, after a terrible attack, as we were sitting having a cup of coffee, I looked at her and said "Elisheva, I hate to see you look like this - your face is still black from fighting the fire in the forest. Are you going to stay on?" She looked at me kindly and said,

"Temima, of course Ill stay. When I came here I dug a hole in the hard, dry earth and put my heart in it and a tree sprang up. I could never leave." It was true. When she was assigned to the tree nursery one day, she discovered that when she touched a plant, it was almost as if grew to twice its size. So, from that time on, she was put in charge of the tree nursery, and every plant flourished.

Elisheva's husband turned out to be Moshe Furmansky, the young man who had arranged for my visit to the Kibbutz. Sadly, he was killed in the war for independence in 1947. In later years, Elisheva remarried. By this time, industrialization of many kibbutzim had begun. A plastics factory had been built in Mishmar Haemek and after some time, Elisheva became the manager and brought to it her skill and dedication. In 1979, on another visit, Elisheva took me to the factory, which by this time had grown tremendously and was manufacturing every conceivable type of plastic, and introduced me with pride to her 24-year-old "boss", the new manager of the factory. Elisheva was now working mornings only, as was the custom for all the older members making room for younger men and women to take over the managerial jobs. This is the way the kibbutz assured itself of continuity. They handed over the responsibility of running the kibbutz to their sons and daughters who then remained in the kibbutz, not leaving it to seek their fortunes elsewhere as was happening in other kibbutzim.

Another thing that impressed me very much about the Kibbutz was the manner in which they handled difficult personal problems. Chana was a real

Elisheva

character. If there was any possibility of a complaint, she managed to find it. She rarely accepted a work assignment from the work committee without grumbling about its unfairness. No assignment was accepted by Chana without an argument. The members were at their wits end. To ask her to leave the kibbutz would have been an admission of defeat. The kibbutz philosophy stated the belief that every human being should be able to live in a cooperative society and learn to share in the daily tasks, simple or difficult, realizing that every effort would be made to be fair to everyone. Chana, however, believed that she was discriminated against and that she was always given the most menial tasks to do. Finally, someone came up with a solution. Chana was put on the work assignment committee. From that moment on there was never a complaint from Chana, no more grumblings, no more long faces. Chana had found her place. She was happy. She was fair. The kibbutz membership breathed a sigh of relief.

CHAPTER 15 - ZVI

During the first few weeks in the Kibbutz, I nothing to do with Zvi, that young man who had offered me his seat on the bus. He was tall and handsome with the perfect features of a Greek god. His thick black hair fell back from his forehead in soft, shining waves. His perfectly shaped dark eyebrows framed deep-set brown eyes. He was very well liked in the Kibbutz not only because of his genial personality but because he was a most willing worker who never turned away from a job, no matter how difficult. Over and above all this, he was an inventive genius. His nickname was "Zvi Patent" because he always found new ways to solve difficult problems.

One of these difficult problems arose one night when Zvi was on guard duty. The Arab village of Abu Shusha, neighbor of the Kibbutz, had recently been infiltrated with terrorists from Syria who forced the villagers to attack their former friends, threatening to destroy the village if they refused. So, every night, there was an attack on the Kibbutz from that direction in addition to the attacks on the forest. This particular night, the volleys came thick and fast. Suddenly, Zvi left his station, ran to the workshop, found a piece of dark stove pipe, returned to his post and propped the stove pipe between two rocks, pointing down in the direction of Abu Shusha. The shooting stopped immediately. In the darkness of night, that stove pipe looked like a real cannon. To the great relief of the chaverim there were no further attacks on the Kibbutz and Zvi was hailed as a hero.

How did Zvi and I finally become good friends? It was customary at the end of the hard working day for the chaverim to find some relaxation by listening to records from a large collection of classical music that friends had sent over the years. The record player was kept in a small shack, where, after the evening meal, the chaverim would gather to listen to Mozart, Bach and Beethoven, trying to forget the problems of the day. This particular evening, the shack was so crowded that I decided to sit out on the grass, under the tree next to the open window and enjoy the music under the stars. As I sat there, alone, listening to a glorious concerto by Mozart, along came Zvi. He said, *"Mutar lashevet?"* (Is it OK to sit down?) So he sat down and we talked for the first time.

We spoke only in Hebrew or in Yiddish since Zvi did not know any English at that time. Despite the problem of language, Zvi did succeed in introducing me to his very deep interest in astronomy. It was easy to learn about the stars because of their brilliance and accessibility. You need only reach out and feel that you could touch a star, it seemed to be so close because of the clarity of the atmosphere. So the stars became a binding interest for both of us, which we followed throughout our fifty years together.

From that time on we met whenever we had free time. I frequently went with Zvi on guard duty had learned not to jump at a rustle of leaves or the falling of a branch. We always had a great deal to talk about. We had come from different parts of the world with differing backgrounds and very different opportunities for education and for earning a living. We talked about our families, the environment in which we grew up, he in a small village in Galicia, and I in the great metropolis of New York City. It was fascinating to discuss and to discover the areas of similarity between us, of which there were many. Then, for "refreshment", we went to the chicken coops where I learned to drink raw eggs, a "cocktail" that I have not imbibed since.

Zvi helped me mount my paintings for my exhibition and built a large frame for the frieze that I had painted for the Children s House as my gift to the Kibbutz. I soon learned of Zvi s interest in cameras. After all, I had brought a moving picture camera with me with which I was to do a film of Youth Aliyah showing how the children, who had been saved from the Holocaust and brought to Israel, had been assimilated into their new environment. So Zvi became my cameraman. However, because of the disturbances in the land, we could not travel to different kibbutzim and youth villages but had to work only with the youth in Mishmar Haemek. I cannot say that we turned out a great film, what with our limited mobility and experience, but I did fulfill my assignment and had something to deliver to the Hadassah Organization when I came back to the United States.

One could never hope to have a more interested audience as were the *chaverim* during the period of the exhibition. Art was the main topic of conversation at mealtime, in the fields, in the showers, in the evening when people relaxed after work on the *desheh*, a tiny patch of grass. They asked many questions, and when those were answered, they asked more questions. What a privilege it was to have such eager learners.

Zvi and I had grown closer and closer. At the time of the grape harvest, he worked hard in the vineyard and at the end of the day, he used to come to the little shack where I was working bringing me a big bunch of the most delicious, green Muskat grapes that were as large as plums. That is how Zvi courted me - with grapes. In later years, whenever, rarely, I found Muskat grapes in some supermarket, we would relish them and remember the grape harvest in Mishmar Haemek and how every night the largest bunch of the largest grapes would be hung from the ceiling in the cooperative dining room for all to see and enjoy with pride.

Now it was time to return home to my work. It was hard to leave the Kibbutz and the many good friends that I had made. Of course, it was very hard to leave Zvi. However, I had to go. Time and distance would have to play a part in the next step in our relationship. And they did. We corresponded, and life went on.

CHAPTER 16 – PAINTING IN MEXICO

Back in New York I busied myself teaching art, painting, lecturing and studying lithography. Then came the summer and I decided to spend it painting in Taxco, Mexico. I rented a little house high on the mountain. Wild orchids and jasmine grew in the garden and the view was breathtaking. My closest neighbors lived either above or below me. Charming houses with gardens dotted the side of the mountain. A little Mexican woman came with the house to clean, shop and cook for me leaving me free to do my work without disturbance.

I spent a wonderful summer in Taxco. I loved to go down into the *mercado* (market) to wander around and sketch. It was so different from any other country I had been to. I enjoyed the stalls with the fresh produce brought from the surrounding areas, the people in their original way of dress. Most of the men wore the wide brimmed sombreros, white smock-like shirts and pantaloons. Women were the workers since many husbands were more interested in a siesta or a long drink of tequila.

You were sure to come across interesting and unexpected characters in the mercado. One day, as I was walking along in, I passed a stall displaying shoes and I noticed a man reading a Yiddish newspaper, the "Forward", the same newspaper that my father read when I was a child. When I greeted the man in Yiddish, he was astonished and delighted. He took me home to meet his wife and children and spent a pleasant afternoon over a cup of tea.

Another day, in the mercado, I met Florence Cane. She was sketching, too. We began to speak. It was the beginning of a deep and lasting friendship. I learned that Florence and her sister were the founders of the Walden School, an excellent, progressive school in Manhattan. Florence Cane was extremely interested in me and practically adopted me as a daughter. I spent many hours with Florence. She was teaching in the Clinic for Gifted Children at New York University under the direction Dr. Harvey Zorbaugh. The children were very talented in art but had emotional problems. Florence was the art teacher, giving the children problems, which relaxed them. She was extremely creative and used scribbles and chanting as well as body movements to help her accomplish this. She was very successful with these methods and I felt very honored when she invited me to teach with her. I learned a great deal from Florence, which helped me greatly in my own teaching later on. This was in 1938.

CHAPTER 17 - RETURN MY LOVE

The summer passed quickly and I was back in New York. I read in the newspaper that El Hanani, a famous Israeli architect whom I had met in Jerusalem in 1934, had come to New York to present his plans for the Palestine Pavilion that he had designed for the 1939 World s Fair. I immediately got in touch with him and when we met, he was so happy to meet a familiar face, somebody who could speak Hebrew, that we sat and talked for hours. He showed me his plans for the Pavilion. I was impressed. His feeling for space, his ideas for presenting the physical, natural, historical, cultural and spiritual aspects of the Land, and an amazing understanding of the materials to be used, held promise for a magnificent result. My appetite was whetted and when I told him that I wanted to be part of this project, he asked to see some of my work. The next day, I brought my portfolio. "You have a good line," he said, "Join us in Tel Aviv and work along with the other artists. You will be paid the same as they." So I started to plan for my third trip to Israel.

I wrote a letter to Zvi to apprise him of my imminent arrival. Imagine my amazement when I picked up the mail the following day and found a letter from Zvi. But it was not an ordinary letter. It was a page torn from a Hebrew book, all greasy and stained with food. It was Rabindranath Tagore's famous poem in Hebrew, *"Shuvi, ahuvati.",* "Return, my love."

How could this have happened? It was only the day before that I had sent my letter. In those days it took three weeks or more for a letter to reach the United

States from Israel. Also, Zvi was not the sort of person who would tear the page from a book. And why was it stained and greasy? Not until Zvi met me as I got off the boat in Tel Aviv a few weeks later, were those questions answered.

Zvi had stopped one evening to buy a *falafel* sandwich, which is the Middle East equivalent of the American hamburger, from an Arab street vendor who did a thriving business. Zvi was one of his regular customers. The vendor filled the filafel sandwich with all the necessary condiments and wrapped it, not in wax paper or a bag, but in a page he tore from a Hebrew book that he had found somewhere. These pages served not only as wrapping paper, but also as reading material during the solitary mealtime. So it happened that Zvi was holding his filafel and the greasy Hebrew page when he discovered that he was reading the famous love poem, "Return, my love!" So he folded the page, put it in an envelope, and mailed it to me in New York. When my boat landed in the port of Tel Aviv, there was Zvi waiting for me.

Zvi always had a great desire to continue studying. He had even thought about studying in the United States. With that possibility in mind he had taken a job in Haifa Port loading crates of oranges on to the ships. He worked the night shift so that he could study at Haifa Technion during the day. His schedule was very heavy, taxing every ounce of energy. But he had a goal and that gave him the spirit to carry on. At six every evening, he would go down to the port, work through the night on the docks, grab a shower and a nap in his room in Hadar Hacarmel, dash off to the Technion for classes, and then return at six p.m. to the ship, ready for another night of loading oranges. Meanwhile, I went to work with El Hanani s artists, making sketches, assisting wherever necessary and doing the numerous tasks that had to be done.

However, everything was eclipsed when Zvi and I decided to get married. We were to be married in the Tel Aviv Municipality city hall in a ceremony officiated by the rabbi of the municipality. We were to bring two witnesses and a wedding ring. The witnesses were readily available, but the ring cost too much. So we decided to rent the simple gold band, and, when the ceremony was over, we returned it and I put on a little, filigree, Yemenite band that I had among my collection of trinkets. I wore that little ring for many years until it wore thin and broke. We replaced it with a gold band reminiscent of the first one.

We arrived at the Municipality and had to wait our turn with quite a few couples who were there for the same purpose - to be officially registered by the rabbinate. The place reserved for marriage ceremonies was quite beautiful. It was in the garden full of exotic trees and flowering bushes. The *huppa* (bridal canopy), was in an arbor completely covered with flowers. The sky was the fresh, cloudless Israel blue, the sun, brilliantly lighting up the hopes of the young people assembled there.

Then came our turn. I wore a simple blue summer dress and white sandals, Zvi, a white shirt, open collar, light gray slacks and sandals. My "veil" was a very delicate, sheer scarf that I had bought in Mexico and

Temima at Zvi - Wedding Day - 1938

which was worn over the head and face for protection from the hot sun. It was very pretty, and it was the reason that we found ourselves having to wait for three more ceremonies to take place, because each of the next three brides begged to be married wearing my "veil." So we were married. The date was August 21, 1938.

CHAPTER 18 – A NEW LIFE TOGETHER

I prepared to return to the New York and Zvi followed a few weeks later, stopping off in Poland to see his parents. He did not give them notice that he was coming and his mother almost fainted when he walked in on her as she was preparing the midday meal. To this day I regret not having gone with him. It would have been wonderful to meet Zvi's venerable father, his very beautiful mother, his two sisters, I did meat his brother Zysio. Unfortunately, I missed that opportunity because I was very dedicated to my teaching and felt that I had to be in the classroom on the first day of school. After surviving several years in concentration camps and displaced persons camps, Zysio and his wife Fanya stopped to visit us in New York en route to their new home in Melbourne, Australia. The rest of family died in the Holocaust.

Now, after praying for me to get married, my mother met her new son-in-law. She was thrilled by his personality, his physical beauty and his fluency in Yiddish, even though it was "*Galitzianer*" Yiddish. We moved into our first little apartment near Prospect Park. The next morning, Zvi took the subway and registered at Columbia University for a course in air conditioning engineering. A few days later, he registered for a course in refrigeration and got a job for ten dollars a week servicing a series of Stewart cafeterias. This was the way Zvi operated all his life. Grass never had a chance to grow under his feet. He got an idea and immediately acted upon it, no matter how difficult. Later, Zvi registered at N.Y.U. in the Engineering Department. After a full day, he would add another few hours at

*Temima at Zvi, with Zvi's brother Zysio
and his wife Fanya, in New York.*

school carrying a heavy schedule and thinking nothing of it. He was finally studying in a university free and unhampered by the european anti-Semitism he had escaped, or anything else! He enjoyed every moment despite the fact that he was working very hard.

I was hired to be the director of the Department of Art Education for the newly formed Jewish Education Committee, now the Board of Jewish Education of Greater New York. An important philanthropist, a man named Rosenauer, had left three million dollars for religious education. One million for Catholic education, one million for Protestant education and one for Jewish education. So the BJE was born, with Dr. Alexander Dushkin as its first director. I had read about this and naturally felt that art should be part of any educational venture from the very beginning. So I wrote a letter to Dr Dushkin asking for an interview. It was granted.

Dr. Dushkin was a very well known educator from Chicago formerly from New York. He had been one of Dr. Benderly s disciples who believed that education was a complete process, which included the arts as well as the academic subjects. He himself played the cello. His brother was a well-known violinist. He was easy to talk to and I presented him with a plan for an art department, which placed serious emphasis on the development of creative teachers. I envisioned a workshop where any teacher could come to learn the use of different media. They would learn to paint, work with clay, handle all kinds of tools, and discover that they had ten wonderful fingers that could create something from nothing. I wanted them to learn that they could learn about their tradition not only from books, but by using all their senses. We talked on and on for several hours.

Then, Dr. Dushkin said, "Mrs. Gezari, I would hire you on the spot, except that there is one more person I must interview before I can make my final decision. I have been trying to get in touch with a young lady who I am told is tops in the field, but I have not yet been able to locate her. After I meet with her, I will let you know my decision."

I was very curious. Who could this other person be? There were very few art teachers in the Jewish field, and I thought I knew everybody. So I asked him, "Do you mind telling me her name, Dr. Dushkin, I might be able to help you find her." He said, "Her name is Temima Nimtzowitz." That was my maiden name! I told him that I was she and that I had married and I was now Temima Gezari. He was overcome with surprise and delight, and I was hired then and there.

And so Zvi and I started our new life together.

END OF PART II

Biographical Sketch

Temima Gezari came to the United States as a nine month old baby. She was born Fruma Nimtzowitz on December 21, 1905 in Pinsk, Russia. She grew up in Brooklyn with her parents Israel and Bella, sister Etta and brother Ruby. The family lived in the back of her father's hardware store on Pitkin Avenue in Brownsville. When things got better they moved to an apartment above the store, which was heated by a coal stove in the kitchen.

Temima graduated from Brooklyn Girls High School in 1921 and the Teacher's Institute of the Jewish Theological Seminary of America in 1925. Her first art teacher was Bulah Stevenson, an inspiring woman who had a great influence on Temima's early development as an artist. She went on to study art at the Parsons New York School of Fine and Applied Arts with Emil Bisttram and Howard Giles (1923-1927), the Educational Alliance in New York with Raphael Soyer (1926), and the Art Students League in New York. She painted with Diego Rivera on his murals at Rockefeller Center (1933). She also studied at Columbia University, the New School for Social Research, and Hunter College.

Professor Mordecai Kaplan had a great influence on her professional life. In 1935, as Dean of the Teachers Institute of the Jewish Theological Seminary, he appointed her to the faculty, where she taught art education and art history for forty-two years. In 1940, Dr. Alexander Dushkin, director of the newly formed Jewish Education Committee asked Temima to be the Director of the Department of Art Education of what is now the Board of Jewish Education of Greater New York, a position she still holds and actively pursues at this writing, after 63 years.

Her book, *Footprints and New Worlds* (Reconstructionist Press 1957), now in its fourth edition, presents her philosophy of child development through her experiences in art with children and adults. She is a prolific artist, and her painting and sculpture are presented in the retrospective book *The Art of Temima Gezari* (Studio Workshop Press 1985).

Books by Temima Gezari

Published by Studio Workshop Press:

    The Art of Temima Gezari   ISBN 0-9616269-0-9

    Now That I'm Ninety-Five   ISBN 0-9616269-1-7

    Art and Education   ISBN 0-9616269-2-5

    I Remember   ISBN 0-9616269-3-3

    Mama, Papa and Me   ISBN 0-9616269-4-1

    Is There a Tomorrow? Yes!   ISBN 0-9616269-5-X

Reprints available through Studio Workshop Press:

    The Jewish Kindergarden
      by Deborah Pessin and Temima Gezari
      (Union of American Hebrew Congregations - 1944)

    Dovidl
      by H. A. Friedland, Illustrated by Temima Gezari
      (National Council for Jewish Education - 1944)

    Hillel's Happy Holidays
      by Mamie Gamoran, Illustrated by Temima Gezari
      (Union of American Hebrew Congregations - 1939)

    Footprints and New Worlds
      by Temima Gezari
      (Reconstructionist Press - 1957)